Relational Pedagogies

Also Available from Bloomsbury

Socially Just Pedagogies, edited by Vivienne Bozalek, Rosi Braidotti, Tamara Shefer and Michalinos Zembylas
Empathy in Education, Bridget Cooper
Dominant Discourses in Higher Education, Ian M. Kinchin and Karen Gravett
Disruptive Learning Narrative Framework, edited by Manu Sharma, Andrew Allen and Awad Ibrahim
Pursuing Teaching Excellence in Higher Education, Margaret Wood and Feng Su
Subjectivity and Social Change in Higher Education, Liezl Dick and Marguerite Muller
Decolonizing University Teaching and Learning, D. Tran
Social Theory and the Politics of Higher Education, edited by Mark Murphy, Ciaran Burke, Cristina Costa and Rille Raaper
Education, Music, and the Lives of Undergraduates, Brent C. Talbot and Roger Mantie

Relational Pedagogies

Connections and Mattering in Higher Education

Karen Gravett

BLOOMSBURY ACADEMIC
LONDON • NEW YORK • OXFORD • NEW DELHI • SYDNEY

BLOOMSBURY ACADEMIC
Bloomsbury Publishing Plc
50 Bedford Square, London, WC1B 3DP, UK
1385 Broadway, New York, NY 10018, USA
29 Earlsfort Terrace, Dublin 2, Ireland

BLOOMSBURY, BLOOMSBURY ACADEMIC and the Diana logo are trademarks of
Bloomsbury Publishing Plc

First published in Great Britain 2023
Paperback edition published 2024

Copyright © Karen Gravett, 2023

Karen Gravett has asserted her right under the Copyright, Designs and
Patents Act, 1988, to be identified as Author of this work.

For legal purposes the Acknowledgements on p. x constitute an
extension of this copyright page.

Cover design: Grace Ridge
Cover image: borchee/Getty Images

All rights reserved. No part of this publication may be reproduced or transmitted in
any form or by any means, electronic or mechanical, including photocopying,
recording, or any information storage or retrieval system, without prior
permission in writing from the publishers.

Bloomsbury Publishing Plc does not have any control over, or responsibility for, any
third-party websites referred to or in this book. All internet addresses given in this
book were correct at the time of going to press. The author and publisher regret any
inconvenience caused if addresses have changed or sites have ceased to exist, but
can accept no responsibility for any such changes.

A catalogue record for this book is available from the British Library.

A catalog record for this book is available from the Library of Congress.

ISBN: HB: 978-1-3502-5670-5
PB: 978-1-3502-5671-2
ePDF: 978-1-3502-5672-9
eBook: 978-1-3502-5673-6

Typeset by Newgen KnowledgeWorks Pvt. Ltd., Chennai, India

To find out more about our authors and books visit www.bloomsbury.com
and sign up for our newsletters.

Contents

List of Figures		vi
Foreword *Stephen Brookfield*		vii
Acknowledgements		x
1	Introduction	1
2	Relationality in Higher Education	21

Part 1 Relationships with Students

3	Vulnerability as Relational Pedagogy	37
4	Authenticity and Trust in Teaching and Learning	51
5	Student–Staff Partnerships as Relational Practice	67

Part 2 Relationships with Others

6	Supporting Others in Higher Education	83
7	Learning from Others	97
8	Becoming, and an Ethic of (Self) Care	109

Part 3 Relationality and the Sociomaterial

9	Things That Matter	125
10	The Wider Webs of Relations	141
11	Conclusions and Directions for Future Research	153

References	165
Index	181

Figures

6.1	Books with 'thing-power'	93
6.2	A departmental shared space	94
8.1	Concept map of PhD thesis – Re-imagining students' becomings: New approaches to thinking and doing transition	119
9.1	Students' reflections upon their learning experience in higher education	128
9.2	Students' reflections upon their experiences of assessment and feedback processes in higher education	129
9.3	A university building lobby	135
9.4	A Lego assemblage depicting academic integrity in higher education	136
9.5	A scrapheap model of inclusivity in higher education	138
9.6	A belonging quilt square	139

Foreword

Stephen Brookfield

One of the most significant illustrations of relational pedagogy in my life happened when I was a new doctoral student. I had been accepted as a doctoral candidate in the department of adult education at the University of Leicester (UK). My application had caught the eye of Henry Arthur Jones, Professor of Adult Education at the university, and he had agreed to supervise my study. My thesis question was this: How do working-class adults with no education beyond secondary school and few, if no, qualifications to their name, become viewed as regional or national experts in their field of endeavour?

At our first meeting, Professor Jones told me something that stopped me in my tracks; namely, that the methodology in my carefully crafted thesis proposal was inappropriate for the problem I was studying, and that my study needed a complete methodological redesign. He spoke of something called 'grounded theory' which, in 1977, was fairly new, and told me that the survey questionnaire I had assiduously developed would not uncover the information I needed to answer my thesis question. In grounded theory, he told me, you begin by doing open-ended interviews with a few of your participants and then, after reviewing what seems to be your subjects' dominant concerns, you decide on the next themes to be pursued.

As someone trained in my master's degree in scientific methodology, and who had written an MA thesis on Charles Booth's massive statistical survey of poverty in London, I was, to say the least, perturbed. Grounded theory seemed to lack rigour. Talk to a few people, then stop to see what you've got before choosing where to go next. How could that be an acceptable PhD research methodology? It seemed amateurish, almost lackadaisical.

As I took the train back home after our appointment, I noticed something interesting in myself. Although some scepticism remained about grounded theory, I felt no resentment, no chagrin at being made to jump through a hoop because of a research supervisor's whim. Instead, I had the sense that Professor Jones was insisting on this change because it was what the study needed and therefore ultimately in my own best interest.

We spent three years as student and supervisor working on my thesis and this same dynamic played itself out several times. I would be fired up with an idea of what to do next and he would challenge me and posit an alternative. In effect, he made my life progressively more complicated by pointing out contradictions and omissions in my work and urging me to read something new, even when I thought the literature review was already sufficient. But I never felt that his doing this was an act of professorial authority designed to show me who was in charge. On the contrary, as the three years passed, it became increasingly evident to me that his suggestions sprang from his carefully attending to my descriptions of what I was trying to do.

I had already been teaching full time for ten years when I was awarded my PhD in 1980, but my experience as a doctoral student has stayed with me over the subsequent forty plus years of my career. Those three years taught me that at its heart pedagogy is relational. I was constantly challenged as a student, and sometimes got irritated at having to change something I had mistakenly thought was fine. But every change my teacher suggested grew out of conversations where he was trying to understand my thinking and help me do what I said I wished to accomplish. My ideas mattered. He took them seriously and I learned to trust his judgments because they were made to serve my own purposes.

In the four plus decades since my doctoral student days, I have been particularly interested in trying to get students, colleagues and myself to think more critically about the dominant ideologies we hold (and the assumptions that flow from these) that frame so much of how we think and act. Most recently, I have been working on how to encourage white members of mostly white organizations and institutions to uncover and challenge the ideology of white supremacy that frames so many institutional actions and policies. Many of the colleagues and students I work with assert that they have escaped racist conditioning, while others are so fearful of saying the 'wrong' thing and being viewed as racist, that they try to stay quiet, under the radar, afraid to ruffle the waters. Under these conditions not to work relationally is inconceivable. Come in posing as the racism-free expert who is going to bring students and colleagues to your point of enlightened racial cognizance and you are dead in the water.

Karen Gravett knows all too well the importance for students of feeling that they matter; that their identities and experiences count for something and that their teachers are striving to take account of these. Simply dismissing a student or colleague as wrong-headed, ignorant or uninformed is no basis on which to help someone open themselves to alternative ideas. Transformational learning teaches us that a basic tenet of working to help someone become more self-aware is knowing as much about them as you can and, on the basis of that knowledge, creating the best connections, links and bridges to new understanding that you can. This is the heart of the connected, relational, approach she adopts.

In this book you will be taken on a journey that explores the dynamics of working relationally. You will be reminded of the need to be vulnerable and the importance of modelling publicly the openness you wish students and colleagues to develop. You'll consider the fragile nature of trust, how delicate it is to build and how quickly it can be destroyed. The theme of what it means to work authentically, as problematic as that may be, is constantly underscored, as is the crucial importance of dialogic approaches. To be in authentic conversation with students and colleagues is a rare thing and Karen guides us in exploring how that process can be encouraged. It's impossible for me to conceive of any kind of relational pedagogy that does not contain a central dialogic element.

But the book goes further than exploring just the dynamics of teaching and learning. We read of the political nature of mattering, of how meaningful connections and partnerships are crucial to any attempt to resist the instrumental reduction of something as beautifully complex as learning to indices and matrices of assessment or audits of 'effective' or 'best' practices. And, unlike other books on these topics, Karen situates her analysis within the material world of objects – of land, buildings, artefacts, space. The processes she examines all occur within physical, spatial and geographical contexts and any true consideration of relationality and interconnectedness has to acknowledge that fact.

So look forward to being challenged and affirmed in the pages ahead.

Stephen Brookfield
Distinguished Scholar, Antioch University
Adjunct Professor, Teachers College, Columbia University
St Paul, MN

Acknowledgements

I would like to thank all of the many colleagues and friends who have supported and encouraged me with this exciting project. This includes my colleagues at the University of Surrey, particularly Simon Lygo-Baker, Ian Kinchin, Kieran Balloo, Naomi Winstone and Marion Heron, who have all supported me in the writing of this book and with their enthusiasm and faith in my project. A specific thank you to Simon Lygo-Baker for contributing to Chapters 3 and 7, and for engaging in such an interesting dialogue within Chapter 7.

I am especially grateful to my colleagues and friends in the wider sector. I wish to express a particular thank you to Stephen Brookfield for writing the foreword which frames this book, and which sets the scene for the chapters to come. I am grateful to friends and colleagues Nikki Fairchild and Carol Taylor for their encouragement and suggestions with useful literature and their collaborative thinking surrounding pedagogies of mattering. I thank colleagues Sarah O'Shea and Rola Ajjawi for their inspiring conversations on student belonging and engagement. I am very grateful to my husband and two daughters for their support. Lastly, I thank my editors at Bloomsbury, for all of their guidance throughout the publication process.

1

Introduction

What does it mean to work, teach and learn in higher education today? And more importantly, what should, and could, it mean? These are fundamental questions that speak to the values that underpin our practice as educators, and that shape the cultures we foster and work within, and the diverse experiences our students have as they engage with university life. Higher education offers a space in which opportunities exist for many to change, learn and develop. It has often been associated with a taken-for-granted idea of education as something inherently 'good' (Pedersen 2015), or with romantic stories of growth and opportunity (Meyerhoff 2019). And yet, higher education can also be a space in which power relations are durable, and where expectations of behaviour and engagement support the few, and not the many.

Higher education also offers an important opening in which educators and researchers are able to explore the interaction between society, social change and the self. This book is about looking at those interactions both in more detail, and from a different approach from that usually adopted in the literature on higher education. I suggest that understanding relationships – connections, mattering, and *relationality* – as fundamental to learning and teaching can offer potential to change the way we experience our work as educators. I suggest that we are inherently relational beings, that we experience a sense of self through relationships with and in relation to other people. I focus upon the role of relationships in education, how we engage in meaningful connections with others and the concept of mattering – how we feel we feel we are valued by others.

However, I also introduce a broader conception of the relational, and of mattering, using these words in multiple and mobile ways. This idea spills over and beyond the focus upon human interactions that are commonly the mainstay of educational research. Instead, I am interested in understanding bodies, objects, spaces and materialities as an interwoven web of relations.

Throughout the book, matter is both who matters – who should be considered and valued – and matter as a material substance (materialities) and materializing force. This includes all the spaces, objects and 'things' of education: laptops, classrooms, pens, desks, campuses, textbooks, teaching resources, assessment briefs, worksheets, buildings – and bodily materialities too. This book considers how attending to *matter*, in both definitions of the word, might be helpful to our understanding of learning and teaching in higher education – and disruptive to our ways of thinking too. Relations and connections are both human-to-human relationships, the interconnection between self and others and the relations we have to and within a much broader, material, world. Matter matters. These are intersecting ideas, and in playing with both I offer a departure from the work on relational pedagogies currently taking place in the sector which tends to be focused on students, teachers and our ability to represent what happens between humans within the learning environment.

I suggest that, in our excitement to attend to the human interactions that underpin learning, and in our attention to the discursive and social aspects of learning, we often overlook those other, material, aspects that matter to ourselves and to our students, considering matter to be simply 'passive stuff, raw, brute, or inert' (Bennett 2009: vii). As Karen Barad explains, 'It is as if there are no alternative ways to conceptualize matter: the only options seem to be the naïveté of empiricism or the same old narcissistic bedtime stories' (Barad 2003: 827). Rather than being inert, I suggest that such 'things' have agency to shape us and our learning, existing and operating within complex entanglements. Or rather, things or materialities do not contain agency in themselves, but agency is constituted in the entanglements of things. As Karen Barad suggests: 'Agency is not an attribute but the ongoing reconfigurings of the world' (2003: 818). Barad continues to explain her view that 'the world is an ongoing open process of mattering through which "mattering" acquires meaning and form in the realization of different agential possibilities' (2003: 817). For Barad, 'intra-action', as opposed to interaction, suggests that the 'self' comes into being in relation with, and through the entanglement of, oneself with others. Intra-action represents an ontological shift from viewing an individual as a bounded body to a body-in-relations:

> reality is not composed of things-in-themselves ... the world *is* intra-activity in its differential mattering ... That is, it is through specific intra-actions that phenomena come to matter – in both senses of the word. (2003: 817)

As such, this book has an ambitious goal: it is designed to be relevant to educators and those working within learning and teaching, whilst also offering ideas for educational researchers, and dealing with a broad intersection of themes that touch upon the philosophy, history, critical theory and sociology of education. Its goal is to experiment with *posthuman*, *sociomaterial* and other theories, but its objective is not 'to affirm an absolute break' from work that has gone before, as is often assumed by critics of posthumanism (Badmington 2003: 15). I am looking not to break, fracture or divide, but to find overlaps and interconnections. I do not deny that human relationships play a hugely significant role in learning and teaching. On the contrary, the book is underpinned by the belief that both human-to-human, and human–nonhuman, interactions matter, within an entangled web of relations. In exploring a broader perspective of learning and teaching that departs from education as simply a humanist project (Pedersen 2015), I consider what we might do with the idea of a more 'radical relationality' (Fraser, Kember and Lury 2005: 3). Within this perspective, objects and humans are not in binary opposition but are composed of 'nothing more or less than relations … relations and relationality cut through and across all spheres' (Fraser, Kember and Lury 2005: 3). Similarly, I examine the notion that 'ethical relationality is an ecological understanding of human relationality that does not deny difference, but rather seeks to more deeply understand how our different histories and experiences position us in relation to each other' (Donald 2009: 6). As such, the book is designed to build upon ideas that may be comfortably familiar, but also to challenge your thinking and take you somewhere new. Just as you are feeling relaxed and comfortable, I want you to experience a sense of the unfamiliar – where might we be going next?

Specifically, in employing ideas of the relational, and of mattering, I want to speak back to cultures of individualism, and instrumentalism, that permeate higher education (and arguably society). Ideals of 'individuality', and notions of the self as 'project', are entrenched, particularly in Western cultures (Giddens 1991; Bauman 2000; Miller 2010; May 2016). For example, Vanessa May argues that, in today's neoliberal world, 'individuality and being the master of one's own fate' are highly prized (2016: 757–8), and Zygmunt Bauman describes a society consumed by the 'incessant activity of "individualising"' (2000: 31). Individualism, and the freedom to pursue one's desires, has become a taken-for-granted value – commonplace, common sense. But, in an extreme form, it can also be seen as corrosive to collegiality. Of course, a great deal has already been written about the neoliberal world alluded to briefly here, and about the tensions academics face in contemporary higher education. For example, in their critique of the 'impact agenda' in higher education, Richard Watermeyer and Michael Tomlinson (2021: 8) describe a pervasive culture of 'competitive accountability' in UK universities, where:

> so much of what has come to characterise the impact agenda is bound with the elevation of the individual as impact superstar and therefore academics as hostage to individualistic and careerist compulsions or other incentivised behaviours, and competitive accountability, therefore, compensating for the frailty of academics' self-concept.

The cultures Watermeyer and Tomlinson describe are not exclusively a UK phenomenon. As Jill Blackmore writes, in 2020 (1332): 'over the thirty plus years that I have been an academic, I have seen Australian universities become as careless of people and values as they have become corporatized,' while Dorothy Bottrell and Catherine Manathunga explore powerfully the changing landscape of neoliberal universities internationally, across two detailed volumes (Bottrell and Manathunga 2019; Manathunga and Bottrell 2019). I will consider this wider context of contemporary universities further in Chapter 2, but suffice to say here, I don't think that the incentivized culture of accountability, individualism and competition described by Watermeyer and Tomlinson is one in which many academics are comfortable within. Certainly, when training to be a teacher and university librarian nearly twenty years ago, my passions for teaching, writing and helping others to learn bore no resemblance to the 'individualizing' and 'incentivized behaviours' described above. These are still not activities I am interested in, or discourses that depict a view of education that I recognize or that is shared by my close colleagues and collaborators. However, the present problems of academia are well known, and have been critiqued to a level that threatens to engulf the reader within a torpor of fatigue. Instead of dwelling too much on the misery, as Carol Taylor (2018: 3) advocates, I'd prefer to

> think beyond and outside dominant representations of higher education as a contemporary time-space damaged beyond repair by neoliberalism, and of HE learning and teaching as irremediably deformed by the marketisation, hierarchization and competition neoliberalism has ushered in.

Like Taylor, I am more interested to think 'beyond and outside'. Specifically, to understand what the impact might be of something else, something different, something relational, for both teachers and students? Excitingly, as Sian Bayne describes, posthuman theories enable us to 'give ourselves greater permission to experiment':

> In terms of our practice as teachers and researchers, we can see this as an incitement to continue to push at the boundaries of educational possibility, and to do so not within an instrumentalised, commodified understanding of education, but rather one which critically explores what it means – in this moment – to be 'connected'. (Bayne 2018)

This book pushes at those boundaries and explores something more connected, affirmative, generative. Something powerful; something relational. In doing so, I play with the multilayered concepts of connection, relations and mattering. How do we connect to others, and what is the impact of connections in higher education – what Susanne Gannon and colleagues (2019) call 'micro-moments'? What does it feel like to feel that we matter? How can we, as educators, find ways to feel valued, and to experience a sense of mattering within an increasingly marketized, metricized system built on the principles of competition, accountability and survival of the fittest? What do connections and mattering look like in the digital university, and how might higher education move from metrics to mattering? There are no easy answers to these questions. But the questions themselves are important. Examining these questions offers cracks, interstices, writings in the margins of the dominant discourses of higher education. As Fraser, Kember and Lury suggest, thinking about relationality can be regenerative: it acts as a 'lure for life, an enticement' (2005: 3). Ideas matter. Notes in the margins can matter.

A History of the Relational in Learning and Teaching in Higher Education

The even more cheerful news is that many educators in universities, both past and present, have been interested in alternative ways of thinking that speak back to discourses that dominate higher education. Relational pedagogies that foreground the importance of relationships within higher education are becoming increasingly prevalent within pedagogy, practice and research, as educators seek to foster a different kind of education and connection with their learners. Of course, the role of relationships within learning and teaching has already had a long and generative history within the literature, and in order to situate this book within its own web of relations, connected intertextually to the legacy of a wider constellation of research, I devote a little time to the history of the relational in higher education here. Relationships have been considered fundamental to higher education for many years. For feminist writer bell hooks, education as the practice of freedom is built on the connections a teacher might be able to make with their students in the classroom, and with the idea of present, embodied, learning:

> I have been most inspired by those teachers who have had the courage to transgress those boundaries that would confine each pupil to a rote, assembly-line approach to learning. Such teachers approach students with the will and desire to respond to our unique beings, even the situation does not allow the full emergence of a relationship based on mutual recognition. Yet the possibility of such recognition is always present. (1994: 13)

In hooks's view, the possibility of a relationship based on mutual recognition is key to inspirational teaching. For hooks these ideas have been founded on the notion of presence, and the ability to connect to one another as interconnected 'whole' human beings.

> During my twenty years of teaching, I have witnessed a grave sense of dis-ease among professors (irrespective of their politics) when students want us to see them as whole human beings with complex lives and experiences rather than simply as seekers after compartmentalized bits of knowledge. (1994: 14)

Relationships are also fundamental to the work of John Dewey, whose work depicts the learner as a social individual and society as an 'organic union of individuals' (2019: 38). Likewise, John Macmurray argued that 'teaching is one of the foremost of personal relations … It must be a relation in which two human beings meet … care for one another, help one another' (1964: 17). Writers in the field of critical pedagogy have also founded their philosophy on the impact of connections and the interplay between relationships and social norms. Paulo Freire has championed the role of dialogue and holistic learning. For Freire, libertarian education 'must begin with the solution of the teacher-student contradiction' (1968: 45), while Henry Giroux (1983) also explores the role of genuine relationships between teachers and students.

Relationships with our students, and with our own selves as teachers, are powerful themes that resonate through the work of Parker Palmer (1983, 1998, 1999). For example, Palmer writes that 'real learning does not happen until students are brought into relationship with the teacher, with each other, and with the subject. We cannot learn deeply and well until a community of learning is created in the classroom' (1983: xvi). He contends that 'good teachers possess a capacity for connectedness' (1998: 11), and he also examines how we might better understand the relationship with ourselves, and why this might matter:

> Why embark on an inner journey in the first place? Because teaching, like any truly human activity, emerges from one's inwardness, for better or worse. As I teach, I project the condition of my soul onto my students, my subject, and our way of being together. The entanglements I experience in the classroom are often no more or less than the convolutions of my inner life … Of course, this focus on the teacher's inner life is not exactly a conventional approach to problem solving in education! We normally try to resolve educational dilemmas by adopting a new technique or changing the curriculum, not by deepening our own sense of identity and integrity. We focus on the 'whats' and the 'hows' of teaching – 'What subjects shall we teach?' and 'What methods shall we use?' – questions that are obviously worth asking. But rarely, if ever, do we ask the equally important "who" question: "Who is the self that teaches? (Palmer 1999: 1–2)

For Palmer, the 'who' question is fundamental, particularly in the understanding of the way that a teacher's selfhood might relate to others.

Viewed from a contemporary perspective, there are a number of possible issues with Palmer's conception of an inner self: concepts of an authentic inner self and 'selfhood' are complex, and have been problematized (e.g. Giddens 1991; Miller 2010). Instead, our complex identities might be understood as constantly in flux and becoming (Gravett 2021). But the key message from Palmer's work – of the value of connectedness – is an idea that can still enrich our teaching today.

Similarly, Gert Biesta (2004) has also written about the importance of relations. Interestingly, here, Biesta contends that learning takes place between the relationship – in the gap – itself between student and teacher.

> Education is located not in the activities of the teacher, nor in the activities of the learner, but in the interaction between the two itself. Education, in other words, takes place in the gap between the teacher and the learner … A theory of education is, in other words, a theory about the educational relationship. It is not about the 'constituents' of this relationship (i.e. the teacher and the learner) but about the 'relationality' of the relationship. (2004: 12–13)

For Biesta, then, what is important is not the inner self of student or teacher, but the 'relational' quality of the relationship itself. Educational relations are both situated and complex, but learning happens in the gap, the interaction. Resonating with these ideas is Stephen Brookfield's work (2015, 2017). Brookfield has also explored the complexity of learning and teaching as well as the significance of meaningful relationships with students, examining the concepts of vulnerability, credibility and trust. Brookfield describes how the most effective teachers 'are also regarded as flesh-and-blood human beings with passions, enthusiasms, frailties, and emotions' (2015: 43). In contrast to these 'flesh-and-blood' beings, Brookfield notes that

> the language of student learning is, on the whole, fairly bloodless. Learning objectives, learning styles, domains of learning, transfer of learning; all these suggest that learning is primarily a cognitive process to do with processing information in various ways. Yet as any teacher knows, learning – particularly that involving risk, discomfort, or struggle – is highly emotional. Sure, there are times when boredom and apathy reign supreme. But there are also times when anxiety, terror, shame, and anger are paramount. Fortunately, too, there are times when students feel joy, pleasure, pride, and love. It is interesting that no assessment protocols I know of make any use of these words or terms like these. (2015: 55)

As we can see, many of these authors refer to the disjuncture between the 'bloodless' discourses of learning, where learning is conceptualized as a cognitive, transactional, process, and their own conceptions of a more embodied, relational pedagogy, involving emotions and passions, and where learning is understood as something more messy, complex and situated. As Biesta and colleagues suggest (2004: 5), 'a fog of forgetfulness is looming over education. Forgotten in the fog is that education is about human beings. And ... we have also forgotten that education is primarily about human beings who are in relation with one another.' The words here are revealing on a number of levels, and I will revisit this quote in a moment.

A similar attention to relationships can be seen within the education literature that has championed an ethics of care, for example, in the work of feminist writers Joan Tronto (1993, 2015), Carol Gilligan (1982) and Nel Noddings (1986). Noddings's work (e.g. 1986, 2005, 2012) foregrounded themes of caring and relatedness within mainstream American literature. Noddings suggests that 'a climate in which caring relations can flourish should be a goal for all teachers and educational policymakers' (2012: 777). Specifically, she writes:

> The academic demands on teachers today are increasingly misdirected. Change is needed, but it will be very difficult. All over the world, thoughtful educators now emphasise the need to place cooperation over competition. This does not mean to eliminate competition entirely; some competition is both necessary and healthy. At its best, it helps us to improve performances and turn out better products. In the 21st century, however, recognition of our global interdependence and a commitment to cooperation must replace the 20th-century emphasis on competition.

We can see therefore that many educational thinkers' writings on education have evolved around concepts of meaningful connections and student–teacher relationships as being core tenets of effective learning and teaching.

In the twenty-first century, a commitment to cooperation may not yet have replaced an emphasis on competition as Noddings hoped; however, an interest in the relational is experiencing a further revival. This is noticeable in a recent work by Peter Felten (2020) who contends that 'relationship-rich experiences' are crucial for students, particularly in view of the increasing diversity of the student body and escalating concerns about student well-being. Likewise, Cathy Bovill (2020a) actively engages the concept of relational pedagogies as ways to build meaningful relationships between staff and students and to offer alternatives to impersonal customer-focused versions of higher education. Relational pedagogy, Bovill writes, 'puts relationships at the heart of teaching and emphasises that a meaningful connection needs to be established between teacher and students as well as between students and their peers, if effective learning is to take place' (2020a: 3). Work by Kirsty Finn (2015) on women's experiences in higher education also examines the role of a relational approach to student experiences. Finn explains that often 'emotions and relational concerns are seen as somehow outside of everyday life at university ... notions of affect and feelings of relatedness become background factors ... rather than the focal point of studies which seek to understand the everyday experiences of student life' (2015: xii).

The importance of relationships, connections and mattering has also been unpacked in the work of Harriet Schwarz (2019). Schwarz reminds us that relational pedagogies are not fluffy ideas: 'relationships are not inherently or essentially light or easy' but 'dynamic and complex' (xiii). For Schwarz, the notion of *mattering* is key: 'When I think back to my most important teachers and mentors I realise that feeling as if I mattered to them was a common thread in all the relationship' and, similarly, 'some of the most memorable and motivating experiences as a teacher have been when I felt I mattered in the lives of students' (2019: 131) Schwarz suggests that even 'one good exchange' can have the power to enrich students' experiences of learning, whilst simultaneously fuelling 'our ability to work' (2019: 27). Interestingly, Schwarz contends that high-quality connections do not have to signify higher workloads for academics or time commitments (2019: 27). This is a criticism commonly levelled at arguments for relational pedagogies, and I will return to Schwarz's work and to these ideas throughout the book. Similarly, the power of relational connections has been further emphasized by Caroline Walker-Gleaves (2019), who argues that creating purposeful relationships is critical to student learning, while Kathleen Quinlan (2016) also argues for the significance of intangibles such as emotions and relationships to be awarded much greater attention in higher education research and practice (Quinlan 2016). Care, and its role within education, has also been explored in other recent work (Barnacle and Dall'Alba 2017; Kinchin 2019; Burke and Larmer 2020).

Moreover, under the umbrella of broader sectoral interests in student-centred learning and engaging students' voices, a substantial body of student engagement literature now exists (e.g. Wimpenny and Savin-Baden 2013; Zepke and Leach 2010), including a dedicated journal, *Student Engagement in Higher Education*. Closely related to this literature sits an expanding body of literature examining the role of working in partnership with students (Cook-Sather, Bovill and Felten 2014; Gravett, Yakovchuk and Kinchin 2020; see also the *International Journal of Students as Partners*). My own work (Gravett and Winstone 2020) has explored the themes of students' connections and relationships via story-mediated interviews with UK undergraduate students. In this study, we found that relational pedagogies position meaningful relationships as fundamental to effective learning and teaching and we explored ways of fostering connections in HE (Gravett and Winstone 2020: 12):

> In particular, we suggest that students need to be understood as individuals with diverse experiences … We also advocate the need to prioritise relational pedagogies, to find spaces for new conversations around relational learning to take place, and for staff to be recognised and supported in their work developing learning.

Relationships and connections between teaching or academic colleagues have also been discussed widely in the literature, for example, Ian Kinchin and Naomi Winstone (2017) who explore how colleagues make use of mentors and critical friends in order to navigate a shifting academic landscape and mitigate the impact of 'pedagogic frailty'. Or Carol Taylor and colleagues (2020) who explore the shared experiences and 'grim tales' of academic colleagues within the neoliberal university. Similarly, Susanne Gannon and colleagues (2019: 48) consider the ways in which academics 'engage in moments of resistance by mobilising resources beyond those of critique', and focus on the 'joy and positive affect in the everyday moments of academic life'. While Marion Heron, Nadya Yakovchuk and I (2020) consider the ways in which academic writers are able to flourish when working with supportive colleagues and engaging in collaborative writing opportunities, despite contexts of performativity.

The literature on this topic is clearly vast; so why have relational pedagogies not been already adopted into mainstream higher education? This is a knotty question. But, firstly, it needs to be stated that relational pedagogies are desperately due further and renewed attention. As has been considered, developing meaningful connections with others, and care of the self, is incredibly hard in contemporary universities where entrenched cultures of marketization and competitive accountability dominate, and where the teaching of large diverse populations may be carried out predominantly by overstretched staff, often on precarious contracts. Relational pedagogies become increasingly important in times which are destabilized and unsettling. The influence of neoliberalism and the marketization of higher education has had an impact on caring relationships, with implications for who can and cannot survive in higher education, meaning that 'attending to difference or indeed developing more expansive forms of care have been rapidly diminishing' (The Care Collective 2020: 4–5). These are themes that are explored further in Chapter 2. Additionally, while the literature has focused on the mattering of teachers and students, or students and peers, I believe that there is a further significant dimension of relationality that has so far been occluded from the discussions surrounding relational pedagogies, and that a broader conception of the relational is required if we are to understand learning and teaching experiences in higher education. Moreover, I contend that this is a frame which holds the power to upend the way that we think about learning and teaching altogether.

Theorizing Materiality and Relationality in Higher Education

As explored in the introduction to this chapter, fundamental to this book is also the idea that connections, matterings and the relational are not just human concerns. Despite the fact that education is often viewed as the 'humanist project par excellence' (Pedersen 2015), I will argue that things matter too; agency is constituted in the entanglement of objects, materialities, spaces and environments. In this sense this book now departs from conventional explorations of relationships in higher education. I am interested in the relationships that we form with our students, and with our colleagues and with ourselves, but I am also concerned with the relational, situated, contexts that we work and learn within and the things that make and impact upon us. And yet, in education at least, material objects 'things' are often overlooked. In his book on material culture, *Stuff*, Daniel Miller (2010: 44) explores the 'somewhat unexpected capacity of objects to fade out of focus and remain peripheral to our vision, and yet determinant of our behaviour and identity ... The objects had managed to obscure their role and appear inconsequential'. Miller adds:

> Objects don't shout at you like teachers, or throw chalk at you as mine did, but they help you gently to learn how to act appropriately. This theory also gives shape and form to the idea that objects make people ... But the lesson of material culture is that the more we fail to notice them, the more powerful and determinant of us they turn out to be. (2010: 44)

Miller suggests that humans want to escape being material, in order to preserve a simplistic view of our humanity:

> Stuff is ubiquitous, and problematic. But whatever our environmental fears or concerns over materialism, we will not be helped by either a theory of stuff, or an attitude to stuff, that simply tries to oppose ourselves to it; as though the more we think of things as alien, the more we keep ourselves sacrosanct and pure. The idea that stuff somehow drains away our humanity, as we dissolve into a sticky mess of plastic and other commodities, is really an attempt to retain a rather simplistic and false view of pure and prior unsullied humanity. (Miller 2010: 10–11)

A much broader concept of human activity as entangled with spaces and things is elaborated in the work of Sara Ahmed, for example, in terms of the power of feminist things (2017) or with regards the impact of spaces and buildings that perpetuate exclusion (2012). Similarly, a broad conception of relationality is articulated by Joan Tronto in her discussion of the concept of care within education:

> In the most general sense, care is a species activity that includes everything we do to maintain, continue, and repair our world so that we may live in it as well as possible. That world includes our bodies, ourselves, and our environment, all of which we seek to interweave in a complex, life-sustaining web. (2015: 3)

Importantly, for Tronto, the relational can be understood to encompass 'our bodies, ourselves, and our environment, all of which we seek to interweave in a complex, life-sustaining web'. There is a need, then, to move beyond the humanist frame that has so far dominated the way in which we view our pedagogy, practice and research.

The need for an expanded perspective has become vividly apparent as a result of the Covid-19 pandemic, and the move to remote and hybrid learning. No longer can we understand concepts such as engagement, agency or connection, in terms of simply what teachers, students or individuals do. Instead, the impact of our access to space; quiet; time; technologies; crucial objects such as laptops, notebooks, screens, chairs, desks and headphones becomes impossible to ignore. The contours of our daily lives are dominated and restricted by objects: masks, lateral flow tests. Engagement in the digital university is not simply a human choice but interdependent with the very materialities and technologies of our situated contexts. To understand how we learn, we need to understand our relationships with each other, ourselves and crucially with the environments and materials that surround us.

This book is therefore an attempt to use a breadth of ideas to think differently, and I suggest that posthuman, sociomaterial and other theories can offer educators new directions in which to understand our practice, and powerful perspectives in which to consider a more 'radical relationality' (Fraser et al. 2005: 3). Posthumanism and sociomaterial theory sit as part of a broad and nebulous theoretical field that also includes relational materialism, feminist new materialism, actor-network theory, spatial theories and postqualitative inquiry. Posthuman theorists include the work of Donna Haraway. Haraway (1988) introduces the concept of 'situated knowledge', based in an inherent relationality with the world and others. Similarly, Karen Barad's work introduces the concept of 'intra-action' (2007). Barad writes that 'nothing exists in and of itself ... everything is always already in relation ... matter and discourse are co-constitutive'. For Barad (2007: 353), 'all real living is meeting. And each meeting matters'. Crucially, posthuman approaches offer new insights which 'extend traditional conceptions about what matters' (Taylor and Fairchild 2020: 1).

Writing this I am conscious that language such as human, posthuman, sociomaterial can be alienating to those who are new to thinking with theories in this way. Posthuman theorists do not mean that humans do not matter, or that material objects and spaces are alive in the same way as humans. Rather, in order to understand learning and teaching more richly, as educators we need to pay attention to the influence of more than just that of student or teacher, as free-floating agents disconnected from the material world. Posthumanism views the human as being in relation – with other humans, other-than-humans and nonhumans. As a result, these ideas also overlap with work that has situated the university within a broader ecological perspective (Barnett 2018) and with the work of sociologists who have explored the role of materiality in society and education (Miller 2010; Brooks and Waters 2019). While there is overlap between these perspectives, in its decentring of human actors, as an approach posthumanism enables a radical rethinking of relationality in educational theory and practice. 'Placing the human in-relation – and attending to the entangled matterings that arise from these relations – offers a fundamental recasting of being, knowing and doing in HE and research' (Gravett, Taylor and Fairchild 2021).

Similarly, sociomaterial theories (Fenwick, Edwards and Sawchuk 2011; Gourlay and Oliver 2018) also offer a broader approach, enabling us to attend to a wider assemblage of forces and actors that matter within the learning interaction. Sociomaterial approaches are closely linked to actor-network theories, or spatiality theories (Latour 2005; Massey 2005). Sociomateriality overlaps with these ideas as well as with related ideas from the field of posthumanism. In general, and despite differences, what sociomaterial theorists and approaches share is a belief that experiences are viewed as embodied, and are seen as socially and materially situated in assemblages of human and non-human actors (Gourlay and Oliver 2018). For example, Fenwick, Edwards and Sawchuk explain:

> Humans, and what they take to be their learning and social process, do not float, distinct, in container-like contexts of education, such as classrooms or community sites, that can be conceptualised and dismissed as simply a wash of material stuff and spaces. The things that assemble these contexts, and incidentally the actions and bodies including human ones that are part of these assemblages, are continuously acting upon each other to bring forth and distribute, as well as to obscure and deny, knowledge. (2011: vii)

What is involved in the relationship, what matters, what is entangled within the learning interaction expands to include tools, objects and spaces, meaning that students and teachers are viewed as situated and entangled within complex and messy networks of the everyday. Sociomaterial theory upholds the importance of materiality in all relations.

> What sociomaterial approaches offer to educational research are resources to consider systematically both the patterns and the unpredictability that make educational activity possible. They promote methods by which to recognize and trace the multifarious struggles, negotiations and accommodations whose effects constitute the 'things' in education: students, teachers, learning activities and spaces, knowledge representations such as texts, pedagogy, curriculum content, and so forth. (Fenwick, Edwards and Sawchuck 2011: 3)

Crucially, sociomaterial approaches do not just ask us to look again at the role of things – contexts, objects, matter – but they suggest that it is the relationality of 'students, teachers, learning activities and spaces, knowledge representations such as texts, pedagogy, curriculum content, and so forth' that we need to understand. As such, sociomaterial theories offer openings that make both the things and the assemblages of education visible in new ways. These fluid and overlapping theoretical ideas underpin this text, and are examined in greater depth throughout the book.

And yet, to date education literature has largely followed a cognitivist and humanist paradigm that has considered relationships between teacher, student and peer, but neglected to look beyond this person-centred frame; within education, who and what matters is almost always understood as human. As Biesta and colleagues explain (2004: 5), 'education is about human beings. And … we have also forgotten that education is primarily about human beings who are in relation with one another'. The relationality of human beings has been neglected. However, what we have also neglected to notice is that education can be viewed through a broader lens, one that decentres the human altogether. Throughout this book then, I consider what ideas can offer our thinking. Specifically, in Part 3, I ask how our understandings of relationships might shift if we disrupt human-centric notions of relations, connections and mattering. Such broader 'pedagogies of mattering' (Gravett, Taylor and Fairchild 2021) can, I suggest, enable us to notice and consider the impact of a wider breadth of actors upon learning and teaching. What might a broader conceptualization of relationality do for our understanding of pedagogies within HE? A posthuman relational pedagogy asks new and challenging questions about how we think about and conceptualize connections, and how we might foster broader ways of thinking about relationships, emotions, space, places, objects, bodies and matter within the learning environment.

Like all scholarship, a posthuman relational pedagogy remains indebted to, and situated within, an intertextual web of existing ideas and literature. Importantly, one contribution that is too often overlooked is that relationality has long been absolutely fundamental to ways of thinking and being within Indigenous cultures (e.g. see work by Donald 2009; Watts 2013; Todd 2016; Wilson 2016; Kimmerer 2020), and Indigenous scholars have raised robust and valid concerns that Western academics often erase Indigenous critical scholarship (Todd 2016). Zoe Todd has argued that any Western scholarship exploring relationality, posthumanism and the role of the more-than-human will inevitably share 'tangled roots' with non-European knowledge systems

(2016: 8), and that these roots should be appropriately, and more commonly, acknowledged.

These roots are important to our understanding. In this extract, Vanessa Watts describes some of the fundamental narratives of Indigenous origin stories and how these ideas have come to shape an understanding of the role, agency and relationality of humans within Indigenous cultures:

> in many Indigenous origin stories the idea that humans were the last species to arrive on earth was central; it also meant that humans arrived in a state of dependence on an already-functioning society. The inclusion of humans into this society meant that certain agreements, arrangements, etc. had to be made with the animal world, plant world, sky world, mineral world and other non-human species. (2013: 25)

As Watts describes, within Indigenous storytelling, humans are understood as being in relation with 'the animal world, plant world, sky world, mineral world and other non-human species'. Similarly, in her book *Braiding Sweetgrass*, Robin Wall Kimmerer (2020) also draws upon the creation story, Skywoman Falling, to offer an alternative origin story of an interconnected world. Likewise, in his writings on how the research practice of Indigenous métissage can be used to reframe how Aboriginal and Canadian relations are informed by Indigenous notions of place, Dwayne Donald (2009: 11) describes how:

> For various reasons, I emphasize land and place as key aspects of Indigenous Métissage and decolonization of curriculum and pedagogy. The most significant reason for this is a fascination with the connectivity between place and identity, and how my ancestors choose to map their territory as a way to express who they think they are. Indigenous place-stories and mapping conventions are expressions of sovereignty that are deeply influenced by wisdom traditions and provide specific examples of how to recognize the land as relative and citizen. I am interested in bringing these insights to bear as curricular and pedagogical considerations because they belie the assumed universality of conventional Eurowestern approaches. I think there is much to be learned about citizenship and the land from holding these two mapping traditions in tension.

Here, an understanding of an interconnected relationality is a key underpinning idea. Donald explains how 'my ancestors choose to map their territory as a way to express who they think they are'. These conceptions of relationality are hugely valuable to thinking about education, resonating with the literatures already discussed in this chapter whilst also, as Donald explains, belying the assumed universality of conventional Euro-Western approaches. The legacy

– and continued contributions and scholarship – of Indigenous thinkers to the theorizing of relationality is something I explore further in Chapter 10, although I attempt to acknowledge the broad intertextuality of ideas recurringly throughout the book.

Ideas and Patterns of the Book

The book is structured into three interrelated parts. Part 1 will focus on the role of student–staff relationships in higher education; the second, the role of relationships between colleagues, other educators and with ourselves; while Part 3 will focus more specifically on the role of the non-human within a wider reconceptualization of the breadth and scope of our relationships and connections. Chapter 2 continues the framing begun here, setting the scene for the book's preoccupations with a discussion of the contextual challenges experienced by teachers and academics working within contemporary universities in the UK and internationally. Chapter 3 looks at the concept of vulnerability and how this can be engaged and used in the classroom, and how it can be important within our relationships with others. This chapter explores practical examples of ways in which teachers might engage vulnerability in order to foster connections, and it also attends to wider societal issues of power, class, race and gender and how these forces impact upon our relationships and upon dialogue. Chapter 4 examines the notions of authenticity and trust and how these might be understood and enacted. It considers how ephemeral the concept of authenticity might be, but also its utility in understanding both our own teaching and our relationships and connections with students. While Chapter 5 examines recent empirical work and literature on student–staff partnership and co-creation in higher education, exploring practical ways that teachers can work in partnership with their students in order to develop connections and foster a sense of mattering.

Part 2 shifts to examine the teacher in higher education: specifically, their connections with colleagues. Chapter 6 explores how we can learn from others. In this chapter, I consider specific practical directions for learning from others, for example, engaging in peer observation, the role and power of learning and teaching conversations, and developing our online and offline networks. I also explore what can be learned from others beyond higher education in order to think more broadly and ethically about our work as educators. Chapter 7 focuses on how we can support ourselves and others through our relationships with colleagues. Meaningful relationships and connections with colleagues can offer powerful moments of resistance to neoliberal ideologies and performative regimes, and I consider how we can support others, seeking to make the most of seeking out micro-moments for connection, through routes such as conversations, collaborations and writing. Chapter 8 follows Parker Palmer's (1998) will to examine our own selves as teachers, and engages the theoretical concept of becoming (Deleuze and Guattari 1987). I consider how we can understand change as ongoing, and explore practically how we can continue to develop ourselves in higher education, through literature, continued professional development and engaging with our discipline.

Part 3 moves to focus specifically upon the non-human and upon understanding relationality and mattering in new and experimental ways. In Chapter 9, I think about what and how objects might matter. I explore learning and teaching and how agency is constituted through the entanglement of things: Lego bricks, clocks, pipe cleaners, spaces within the university campus. I consider what happens when we unsettle the rigid boundaries between human and non-human that have long served educational researchers. Chapter 10 draws together the discussions of the many diverse interpretations of relationality. Here, I explore what insights and implications can be taken forward from this rich perspective as we begin to understand ourselves as entangled within a web of relations, and to understand the messy contexts of learning and teaching. I propose ways of conceptualizing relationality that move beyond a conventional humanist perspective, prompting new questions about concepts such as agency, engagement, voice, as well as how we intra-act ethically with one another and with our environments and contexts. The book closes by considering ways in which educators can take this reimagining forward within policy, research and practice. I consider future agendas for research, including research methods, theories and approaches, and I examine new directions for understanding connections, relationships and mattering in higher education.

Conclusions

This book will offer a unique perspective. Moving beyond the traditional cognitive, humanist frame that is normally adopted within education, I contend that the relational encompasses humans, materialities, systems and spaces within an entangled web of relations. Ultimately, I argue for the need to understand the situated, contextual and messy nature of learning and teaching – that cannot be reduced to simplistic performance metrics. Drawing upon a rich assemblage of theoretical lenses, I consider the themes of relationality and relationships from a diversity of intersecting angles. I share practical examples, stories, dialogues and ideas, and these practical ideas will also jostle with theory. A pervasive theme is the intertwined nature of theory-practice as I believe that a theoretical perspective is essential if we are to enact meaningful relational pedagogies that attend to the diversity and materiality of our experiences of higher education.

Sociomateriality and posthumanism may be ideas you are familiar with, or for some readers these ideas might feel unsettling. They may be something that you become intrigued by and want to learn more about, offering new openings for how you think about your research and practice in higher education. You may wish to take the parts that you feel are most accessible and useful to you – although I hope that some discomfort will be pleasurable. The book is written with a view that the reader should not feel they have to read it in a linear fashion but should dip in and out of sections and ideas as they wish. Recurrent themes interweave rhizomatically throughout the text and across different chapters. Readers should feel free to read the text, to visit and return as they feel is useful, at particular points in their career and as thinking evolves. For me, I find meaningful this comment from Elizabeth Adams St Pierre about how thinking does, and should, evolve:

> If we can't think outside what we studied 20 years ago … how can we keep moving, keep thinking, keep inquiring? I think the mark of excellent scholarship is changing our minds and being willing to do that. I tell my students how precarious our work should be, that we should understand that the next article or book we read might very well upend everything we believe and that that is mark of 'rigorous' scholarship. Patti Lather said something about the value of 'rigorous confusion', and I really like that. (St Pierre 2015: 16)

I hope you enjoy this 'thinking outside' and are able to connect some of the thoughts and ideas of the book to your own pedagogy, practice and research, thinking about what matters to you.

2

Relationality in Higher Education

Introduction

Thinking and writing about higher education is a messy and complex endeavour. Universities have long been understood as situated within an age of supercomplexity (Barnett 2000), and as having evolved radically as a result of a myriad of complex societal and economic forces including technology, globalization and the influence of government policies and neoliberalism. Anthony Giddens (1991: 122) has argued that as the pace of social and technological change continues, throwing off unanticipated consequences, contemporary societies can be understood as dominated by unprecedented complexity and risks. Higher education in the UK today also represents a dizzyingly vast breadth of institutions, staff and students. This messy picture is fractured further when we look at the diverse experiences of staff, students and institutions internationally, and further still when we begin to think about education as a situated practice, or as Karen Barad suggests, the world itself as 'a dynamic process of intra-activity in the ongoing reconfiguring of locally determinate causal structures with determinate boundaries, properties, meanings, and patterns of marks on bodies' (Barad 2003: 817). As a result, in this chapter, and in this book as a whole, I'm going to attempt to avoid generalizations or sweeping statements. Moreover, this book is also not intended to offer just another stultifying story of the downfall of universities as a result of neoliberalism. Instead, I will attempt to offer an overview of some of the discourses, and multiplicities, we can observe within the contemporary higher education landscape, in order to understand the diverse contexts of the relational, and how relational pedagogies might play out in universities. In order to sketch a picture, however patchy, of how we might begin to think about relationality and higher education, and to better understand the interplay between policy, discourses and learning and teaching practice, I attend to three pervasive and interwoven tropes that shape the landscape for universities today: higher education as product; the student experience; and the idea of the individual.

Higher Education as Product

A dominant and materializing discourse that has become ubiquitous within today's discussions regarding universities is the idea of higher education as a product to be bought and sold, and of students as consumers. It has been argued that higher education has been, or risks becoming, irrevocably 'deformed' as a result of the forces of 'marketisation, hierarchization and competition neoliberalism has ushered in' (Taylor 2018: 372). Certainly, the function and role of universities, and what they have to offer society, has fundamentally shifted. Today, universities are much more likely to be described as businesses, as entrepreneurial, corporate or enterprising. As a result, they have been depicted as entrenched in academic capitalism, distorted by audit culture, governed by managerialism and even toxic (Bottrell and Manathunga 2019: 2). Within the neoliberal university, the student is positioned, and discursively constructed, as an individual self-governing agent: a customer.

Of course, such discourses are not benign. Discourses matter in so far as that they are significant, but they also matter in that we can understand that words have materializing power over individual subjectivities, shaping the ways in which we understand ourselves and one another (Kinchin and Gravett 2021). Within neoliberal narratives that depict higher education as a product to be consumed, academics and teaching professional staff become assets: valued for their measurable impact within performance management regimes that foster a culture of individualized performativity, 'competitive accountability' and 'agency theft' (Watermeyer 2019: 1). So how did we get here? And why did we let this happen? Evidently, then, we cannot understand contemporary universities without devoting a little time to sketching a history of the encroachment of market forces upon higher education. Perhaps not least because Julie Rowlands and Shaun Rawolle suggest that writers frequently use the word neoliberalism 'as a catch-all for something negative', without offering any meaningful explanation, and that by doing so, 'rather than interrupting the implementation of neoliberal policies and practices, we may, in fact, be further entrenching the neoliberal doxa' (2013: 260). But I do not want to get downhearted – there is something more optimistic coming too.

In their rich and detailed exploration of the impact of neoliberalism upon higher education, Dorothy Bottrell and Catherine Manathunga (2019: 1–2) contend that

> under the ethos of neoliberalism universities have been transformed. In Australia, the alignment of higher education provision with neoliberalism began in the 1980s, as successive governments advocated the need to boost efficiencies, productive competition and public accountability, all deemed lacking within the system of university self-governance. The economic logic of reform ran counter to dominant conceptions of universities as collegial institutions concerned with public and democratic purposes. The dominance of market-driven business models instituted by governments through regulatory regimes and a volatile, mainly lean or declining funding policy environment has similarly reshaped higher education in variegated yet consistent ways in the global north and south.

Here, Bottrell and Manathunga describe the reshaping of higher education under the guise of economic logic, and how this has occurred in 'variegated yet consistent ways' across institutions in the Global North and South. Likewise, Mark Olssen (2016: 129) examines the UK context, starting from a similar period:

> The changes to higher education inaugurated in Britain in the 1980s, as a result of the election of Thatcher's Conservative government, ushered in a sea-change of how the public sector was to be managed, and of the role of government in relation to public spending. The broad faith in Keynesian demand-management, was replaced by a range of new economic, financial and administrative perspectives whose central common assumptions can be seen as constituted by a particular strain of liberal thought referred to most often as 'neoliberalism'. The central defining characteristic of this new liberalism was based on an application of the logic and rules of market competition to the public sector.

As Bottrell and Manathunga explain above, the changing position of universities runs 'counter to dominant conceptions of universities as collegial institutions concerned with public and democratic purposes'. Rather than being underpinned by notions of democracy, collegiality and public good, within a neoliberal ideology, education is conceptualized instrumentally. Similarly, as Olssen contends, a neoliberal ideology is 'based on an application of the logic and rules of market competition to the public sector'. Neoliberalism, then, 'promotes the supremacy of the market, competition, rational choice, the global knowledge economy' (Bamberger, Morris and Yemini 2019: 204).

This undeniably has profound effects upon the students and staff who learn and work within the neoliberal university, and particularly upon how we think about our relationships and connections to one another. As Richard Watermeyer (2019: 4) explains,

> A pressure to perform and satisfy the economic and societal expectations of a marketized ... system of higher education engenders among academics – and certainly their institutions – forms of behaviour that are antagonistic to archetypal ideals of scientific practice yet are excused or obfuscated on the basis of political pragmatism and expediency.
>
> A culture of competitive accountability stimulates performance based anxieties that are corruptive to academics' self-concept.

According to Watermeyer, the modern university has fostered forms of behaviour that are antagonistic to ideals of scientific, or academic, practice; little wonder, then, that academics may experience the new expectations placed upon them as 'corruptive to their self-concept'. In a memorable summary, Watermeyer contends that the university has shifted from 'bastion of intellectual endeavour to engine room of capitalist enterprise' (2019: 2). And yet, of course, the engine room of enterprise is not experienced uniformly. Rather, in a neoliberal culture, survival of the fittest prevails. Precarious contracts for staff are now commonplace, and pressures and expectations are experienced very differently by different groups. Female academics, who are more likely to have caring responsibilities, and are less likely to be able to be geographically mobile; academics from Black, Asian and minority ethnic backgrounds; academics from working-class backgrounds; disabled academics – all are likely to be less able to compete (or survive) upon a neoliberal stage. These pressures have only become more acute as a result of the impact of Covid-19 with labour spread even more unevenly across the neoliberal university (Newcomb 2021).

For students, the impact of this radical sectoral change may be no less profound. As David Harvey explains, neoliberalism 'proposes that human well-being can best be advanced by liberating individual entrepreneurial freedoms and skills within an institutional framework characterized by strong private property rights, free markets and free trade' (2005: 2). The implications being that the student consumer is framed as a liberated individual, this conception altering the nature, purpose and values of HE (Naidoo and Williams 2015). The interpellation of students as 'consumers of educational products' (Ingleby 2015: 518) can be seen to act as a transformative force, altering the very values of education. One impact of this is that, over recent years, the values and purposes of higher education has also become closely intertwined with notions of graduate attributes and an employability agenda. This has been explored by Rachel Brooks, whose study of policy documents across six European nations surfaces how students are constructed recurringly within a 'future worker' discourse 'foregrounding understandings of students as a "worker-in-the-making"' (Brooks 2021: 166). And yet, Jeannie Daniels and Jennifer Brooker (2014) have shown how graduate attributes are hugely problematic, since they focus firmly on students' future identity as workers, rather than enabling students to focus on/enjoy their current identity as students, and in doing so they offer a simplistic, and – for some – troubling, view of the purpose of universities.

Explorations and depictions of the neoliberal context are plentiful in the literature. However, there are nuanced and critical perspectives too. It is certainly possible we have fallen victim to the common mistrust of the present/future in favour of a rose-tinted past that may have never even existed. Carol Taylor (2019: 5) warns us to be mindful of the inequities and challenges that have long plagued higher education:

> I wonder if such a lamentable situation is less a description of a general condition and more a partial perspective capturing a certain sort of melancholia – a euro/western, leftist, white, masculinist melancholia? Perhaps the nostalgia for a better state of being is less about loss and more about a complicated entanglement in which those who were formerly central to shaping a certain sort of (neo-colonialist) discourse about the role of intellectuals in public life now find themselves uncomfortably placed and jostling for position with those 'others' who have (always) been peripheralized within the humanist (masculinist) university.

While she does not minimize the challenges of contemporary universities, here, Taylor reminds us of the danger of partial perspectives, and highlights that it is not only now that certain academics have found themselves on the outside of the humanist, masculinist university. Likewise, Watermeyer too warns of the hindrances of our own biases when seeking to describe contemporary cultures in higher education, and asks: How much might our views be influenced by a bias 'born of nostalgic indulgence?' (Watermeyer 2019: 1). But there is no disguising the seismic changes that have taken place within the sector, and the far-reaching effects of these changes upon the way that both staff and students experience higher education.

The Student Experience

One further outcome, occurring as a result of the changes described above, and of higher education's increasing conceptualization as product, is a dominant focus on the notion of 'the student experience' that has pervaded the language of higher education, policy and practice in recent years. Calls to listen to 'the student voice', to improve 'the student experience', and to monitor and measure how students think, feel and engage with the university have all become what it means to work in a university today. Discursively, this idea is visible in the government White Paper, The Future of Higher Education (DfES 2003). Students are constructed as consumers who are 'entitled to be taught well' (2003: 47). The report states that students are expected 'to become intelligent customers of an increasingly diverse provision, and to meet their own increasing diverse needs'. In her work examining higher education policy, Duna Sabri (2010: 197) identifies the problems associated with this kind of construction of students and their experiences of education:

> 'The student experience' has become a ubiquitous phrase in higher education policy discourse and specifically in discussions of what higher education is for. It is now used as a singular reified entity. 'Student' becomes an adjective describing a homogenized 'experience' that is represented in league tables, such as that produced by the UK National Student Survey. There is no scope to problematize who is a student, where and when this 'experience' stops and starts, how it comes about, how it changes etc. ... A reified 'student experience' is wielded as a criterion for judgement about what is and is not worthwhile in higher education. It demands the exclusion and silencing of other accounts of higher education.

As Sabri powerfully articulates, this homogenized and reified student experience is problematic. Purportedly representative, but essentially meaningless, ultimately the limiting conception of a single student experience demands the exclusion and silencing of alternative accounts of higher education within one overarching 'voice': a voice from above; a voice from nowhere. Rather, students, like all people, have multiple, contradictory, shifting and evolving voices and experiences that can be understood and interpreted in multiple ways. Sabri reminds us of the potency of language:

> language is used to structure the subjects of higher education policy (through rules and resources) rather than to communicate with them. ... The dominance of 'the student experience' in this assumptive world privileges one discourse of higher education learning over possible alternatives. This dominance is recursively

produced in countless university professional development courses that have become compulsory for newly appointed academics in the UK which have to be accredited by the HEA according to its own formulated professional standards. This authoritative resource is re-enforced by the compulsory institutional subscriptions to HEA as opposed to voluntary individual membership, thus re-enforcing the role of the institution as provider. Furthermore, the approaches to learning/student experience literature adopts a perspective that is consonant with the notion of the student as customer. (2010: 201)

Understanding the diverse and evolving experiences of students as individual people beyond the discourses of satisfaction, measurement and marketization has become imperative. But, here Sabri warns that the silencing and homogenizing of more nuanced voices has been harnessed for professional development purposes, and that it has also been exacerbated by popular themes in the educational literature, for example approaches to learning. Similarly, Karen Smith suggests silencing can also be strategically used for policy purposes. Smith's work (2008) analyses the learning and teaching strategies of UK institutions, and shows how both staff and students are surprisingly largely absent from these documents or shown to have low agency. Sabri examines how as a result of these absences, the policy arena becomes 'a distant macro-phenomenon whose characteristics and mechanics only become visible at the institutional levels,' whereas 'the world of policymaking should surely be treated by researchers as a place where micro interactions matter' (2010: 193).

Micro-interactions do and should matter; and it is this point that leads us back to the purpose of this book. Individuals matter: their voices, experiences, preferences, thoughts, actions, connections and relationships – despite the prevalence of dominant discourses that might fail to listen. Other recent work has attempted to engage with students' voices at the micro-level in all their multiplicity and diversity. Simon Lygo-Baker, Ian Kinchin and Naomi Winstone (2019) critique the single voice 'fallacy', advocating a move towards a richer and more meaningful exploration that shifts the gaze from voice to voices. They also explore the potential of projects carried out in partnership with students to engage students as co-creators of their experiences of higher education (a topic explored in further detail in Chapter 5). Similarly, a study using story-completion methods, by myself and Naomi Winstone (Gravett and Winstone 2019), surfaced the varied and micro-experiences of students in transition, as well as the importance to students that their diverse experiences be recognized. In this study, participants reported that they felt alienated by homogenizing phrases such as we are all in 'the same boat' and desired, meaningful, individual connections with peers and tutors. Research projects like these offer irruptions to dominant discourses of students as consumers and reject overarching ideas of the singular student voice or experience. Rather, students can be understood as much 'more than customers' (Gravett, Kinchin and Winstone 2020), and institutions become spaces where relational connections matter and are made possible.

Individual Agency

A further interconnected idea that has also emerged from the neoliberal context, and discourses detailed above, is the notion of individualism and individual agency. Paradoxically, while we have seen that students may often be homogenized by dominant discourses that depict absent students, uniform experiences and singular voices, conversely, we can also see that students are more than ever before expected to act as individuals, to express individual agency and free rational choice, unconstrained by social or economic limitations. As customers, students are often discursively interpellated as individuals whose task is simply to choose well, as evinced in this speech on social mobility from government minister for education (Michelle Donelan 2020). During this speech, Donelan contends that 'true social mobility is about getting people to choose the path that will lead to their desired destination'. Here, the emphasis is firmly placed upon an individual's agency, their ability and responsibility to choose the path 'that will lead to their desired destination'. Students are expected to follow their 'desire', which again reiterates the agency and choice available to the individual, and the explanation is given that such choices are indicative of a more authentic, 'true' mobility. Within this narrative, the appeal to notions of choice, desire and truth interpellate the student into a discursive position where they are imbued with individual agency and possibility. Such a freedom is highly seductive – students are agents of their own fate. The implication is that any deviation from the 'correct' path would be the responsibility, actions or choice of the individual.

Andrew Wilkins and Penny Jane Burke have also explored the role of individual agency and discourses of consumerism in their critique of the narratives surrounding widening participation. They argue that students have become positioned as empowered consumers in pursuit of individual desires (2015: 440); again, we see the depiction of students as homogeneous, 'a single governing norm':

> Canonical concepts that are particular to WP discourses (including choice, empowerment, aspiration and achievement, to name a few) are sometimes

abridged through government texts and policies into a single governing norm: … students as self-governing, 'willing selves' … acting within a pre-determined horizon of thinking and behaviour. (Wilkins and Burke 2015: 436)

We can see, then, that neoliberal discourses of individualism construct students as 'self-governing, willing selves'. And yet, such discourses which centre on an agentic individual, free from the constraints or affordances of social or material contexts, are limiting and exclusionary. Just as discrimination and inequalities remain within society, narratives that focus on empowered individuals are deeply problematic: aspiration is offered 'in ways that adhere to the hegemonic neo-liberal ideal of the entrepreneurial competitor-individual, de-meaning and de-valuing "other" personhoods' (Lumb and Burke 2019: 215). For those who do not achieve, or cannot compete, the assumption is simple: the wrong choices were made.

Similarly, Carole Leathwood (2006) highlights that neoliberal ideas of individuality, employability and productivity have also led to a problematic focus on the notion of independence. The concept of student independence is problematic, Leathwood suggests, as it is gendered and culturally specific. It reinforces 'masculinist myths': 'what suits (some) men is defined as the ideal that all should be striving for, whilst men's dependence on others remains hidden' (2006: 630). According to Leathwood, this construction has practical consequences; because dependence is denigrated, students are reluctant to ask for help or attend special classes, as these signify lack or deficiency. Such individuality narratives can be seen to be firmly entrenched within the 'ethical cul-de-sac' of humanism (Taylor 2018: 82). Taylor explains that what is particularly problematic is 'the relation humanism sets up between the individual and the universal. Humanist ethics locates moral conceptions in individual human bodies while, at the same time, positioning ethics within abstract, universalising and human rights-based discourses' (2018: 83). We can see such an 'individual-universal duality' within the dominant discourses examined in this chapter. Such discourses place the onus upon the individual to succeed, regardless of the broader, contextual factors that impact upon and constrain human agency, and that conflict with ideologies of social justice.

Beyond the Crowd

This chapter has so far painted a bleak picture. However, there is cause for optimism, and maybe even hope. Gaps, contradictions and openings always exist with opportunities for new ways of thinking and doing. For example, Wilkins and Burke believe that

> neoliberalization never fully constitutes the performative capacity of those it directly addresses and seeks to constitute in its own image. A corollary of this is that policy enactments can be understood as terrains for the struggle over meaning and where concepts can be re-imagined. (2015: 449–50)

Concepts can be re-imagined and transformed, and they evolve over time. Certainly, many of the authors cited above have also examined how we might re-imagine, in order to live more liveable lives in higher education, between the 'cracks' of the encroachment of neoliberalism (Bottrell and Manathunga 2019). Bottrell and Manathunga explore the multiple 'resistances' that are taking place in the academy, specifically how

> academics are seeing through the cracks and contesting neoliberal purposes with very different cultural logics and values. … Speaking out, collegiality and collaborative work are necessary practices for 'common good' university purposes. … In many ways, critical pedagogy, collegiality and creative, community focused collective work has morphed into resistance, as opposition to the market imperatives with which managerialism bombards us. (2019: 311–18)

As Bottrell and Manathunga explain, spaces for meaningful resistance exist where different cultural logics and values can be held and lived by. Similarly, Watermeyer contends that it is through following values of collectivism and collegiality that 'the potential for renewal exists'. For Watermeyer, this can occur 'only where academics resist the individualistic impulse of their neoliberal indoctrination and regain an understanding of an empathy with the importance of their collective endeavour' (2019: 142), and when academics break 'the bonds of a competition fetish' (Watermeyer 2019: 142). Speaking out, thinking critically and working collegially may offer spaces for hope and possibility.

There are also further opportunities for alternative perspectives if we look more closely at students' subjectivities. Multiple recent studies have demonstrated that students do not see their university education in economic terms, despite what policymakers might espouse (Lygo-Baker, Kinchin and Winstone 2019; Brooks et al. 2020; Gravett and Winstone 2020; Gravett, Kinchin and Winstone 2020). Instead, many students often want to be perceived as more than customers and may commonly hold values such as community, partnership and dialogue to be important to their learning. Rather than focusing solely on concerns such as employability, or value for money, on the contrary, meaningful interpersonal connections have become of paramount importance to many students (Gravett and Winstone 2020). As Emily Danvers (2021: 4) contends, 'despite this presence of consumerist, individualised and instrumental student subjectivities, the academy is simultaneously and inseparably alive with more recognisably "deconstructive" criticality'.

This deconstructive and vital criticality is exciting. Attempts to foster meaningful connections between staff and students, and students and their peers, offer a critical retort to the neoliberal narratives of higher education, reasserting some of the values potentially jettisoned within a marketized ideology. Individuals matter. Attending to the micro, and to the value of micro-moments between one another can be a powerful opportunity to connect. As Harriet Schwarz (2019) contends, one good interaction between individual teachers and students can be all that matters in making someone feel valued and enabling them to learn and persist, and this is something explored further in Chapter 4. While similarly, the work of Susanne Gannon and colleagues (2019) shows how micro-connections between colleagues can harness feelings of joy and positive connection that can buffer the strains of the neoliberal forces afflicting academics' daily working lives. Crucially, this attention to the individual, this mattering, takes place within a community – not an individualized, competitive arena.

There are further positive developments in the wider higher education context. Widespread work across the sector to decolonize the university, and ongoing debates about anti-racism and gender equality, have signified a move to rethink the wider relationality of institutions with their past, and with societal values, creating discursive and political spaces in which staff and students are able to rethink our relationality in new ways. Theoretically, posthuman, new materialist and sociomaterial turns in the social sciences are starting to gain ground in higher education research meaning that human exceptionalism is being radically critiqued. These theoretical perspectives offer new approaches which enable educators to conceptualize students and staff in more nuanced ways, beyond discursive descriptions of agential individuals or consumers. In the following extract, Taylor describes the openings that posthuman pedagogy, practice and research might offer:

> Posthuman pedagogy, practice and research is all about those 'and-yets', those escapes, being open to them when they arise, riding on them and with them, co-creating them, giving them space to happen, attending to them, and embedding them in curricula, materials, methods, and intra-actions, so that, as teachers, researchers and learners, we can attend in more nuanced ways to what

matters (and how and why and to whom and when). Tending towards the 'and-yet' as a mode of joyful life-affirming 'doing otherwise' in higher education can then help support us to think beyond and outside dominant representations as a contemporary time-space damaged beyond repair by neoliberalism. (Taylor 2019: 6–7)

For Taylor, posthuman pedagogy, practice and research is about escapes, about doing otherwise and about finding new ways to think beyond and outside.

With many overlapping ideas, sociomaterial theories also offer opportunities to speak back to the homogeneous and absent student that we have seen depicted via narratives relating to 'the student experience'. For example, the work of Tara Fenwick, Richard Edwards and Peter Sawchuk (2011), and Lesley Gourlay and Martin Oliver (2018) attends to the significance of the social and the material in order to focus on the situated, diverse, fine-grained, day-to-day practices of students as they engage in higher education. This work offers a means to think and to research learning and teaching differently, attending to the granularity of the everyday micro-experiences of learning, and seeking to trace a more diverse and nuanced account of higher education. Crucially, in its surfacing of the role of the material within learning and teaching, and of the materiality of experience, sociomaterial approaches enable the ordinary objects, things and devices of education to move beyond being simply understood as tools. Instead, materials are understood as having agency via their entanglements with others and things, within networks or assemblages. Again, these ideas offer new ways to understand the day-to-day engagements of learning and teaching, and to speak back to neoliberal notions of future workers or isolated individuals, via a situated focus on the relational present. This builds upon other related theoretical fields, for example spatiality theories, actor-network theory or sociological perspectives on material culture (e.g. Massey 2005; Miller 2010; Brooks and Waters 2019), which have also reignited interest in the role of objects and in material culture.

This book too then follows the call to 'think beyond and outside' (Taylor 2019: 6–7), to consider what else might be possible in our thinking about education. What might be missed within taken-for-granted narratives about how students learn and how teachers teach? Posthuman, sociomaterial and other related theoretical perspectives can be useful approaches in helping us to refocus, attending anew to what might matter, and how we might reconnect to one another thinking beyond and outside some of the neoliberal discourses described and discussed in this chapter. A focus on relationality fosters an understanding of oneself as existing within a broad web of entangled actors, reliant, interdependent and interconnected to one another. In revaluing and reconsidering the notion of dependence and entanglement, such an idea speaks back to notions of an agentic, self-governing, individual that we have seen too often excludes spaces for others to matter, or for many to live liveable lives in the academy, and it is these ideas that underscore the chapters in this book.

Conclusions

This book speaks back to some of the dominant discourses in higher education and seeks to offer something new. It continues important work that has been burgeoning in the sector, work that has begun to prioritize meaningful relationships with students and their peers, with staff and colleagues or with students and teachers, in order to move beyond the dominant discourses of marketization and individualization. And yet, it also goes a step further. I suggest that through thinking with the notion of relational pedagogies, and with the concept of mattering, and by using posthuman and sociomaterial theories to understand ourselves as situated within a web of actors, we can move beyond the deficit conception of isolated individuals. Vivienne Bozalek and colleagues (2021: 1) also examine ways to speak back to individualist discourses in higher education. Putting to work the concept of an ethics of care, they consider how this can be associated with posthuman theory: 'both the political ethics of care and posthuman ethics redefine the values and practices of care, providing ways of moving beyond liberal individualist approaches that are grounded in Enlightenment ideas'. A posthuman inflected perspective pushes back against the notion of human exceptionalism and agency, and asks what a wider conception of the relational might offer us in order to think differently about the value of connections, and what may be lost when individualism is prized. Instead, this book's perspective reprioritizes values such as connectedness, relationality, collegiality, community, the micro, mattering and entanglement. This thinking takes place in the cracks that Bottrell and Manathunga describe (2019), and offers a source of activism.

Part 1
Relationships with Students

3

Vulnerability as Relational Pedagogy

Introduction

Here is a secret hidden in plain sight: good teaching cannot be reduced to technique; good teaching comes from the identity and integrity of the teacher. In every class I teach, my ability to connect with my students, and to connect them with the subject, depends less on the methods I use than on the degree to which I know and trust my selfhood – and am willing to make it available and vulnerable in the service of learning … teaching is a daily exercise in vulnerability. (Palmer 1998: 72)

A good teacher must stand where personal and public meet, dealing with the thundering flow of traffic at an intersection where 'weaving a web of connectedness' feels more like crossing a freeway on foot. As we try to connect ourselves and our subjects with our students, we make ourselves, as well as our subjects, vulnerable to indifference, judgment, ridicule. To reduce our vulnerability, we disconnect from students, from subjects, and even from ourselves. We build a wall between inner truth and outer performance, and we play-act the teacher's part. Our words, spoken at remove from our hearts, become 'the balloon speech in cartoons'. (Palmer 1998: 67)

This chapter considers relationships between students and teachers, focusing in particular upon the idea of vulnerability in learning and teaching. In his influential work included above, Parker Palmer discusses the importance of the identity and integrity of the teacher, encouraging us to consider carefully our own identities. For Palmer, good teaching cannot be reduced to technique. Rather, he explains that his ability to connect with his students depends much more on the degree to which he is willing to make himself vulnerable, and that for him this is 'a daily exercise'. When I first came across Palmer's work, his ideas about focusing inwards, in order to connect outwards, really resonated with me. For many years, I had felt dissatisfied with a predominant focus on technique within the contexts in which I taught, an attention to the tips, tricks and technologies of teaching that I saw in both practice and in the literature. The kinds of questions being asked seemed to be the following: if I record my lectures will that be the solution to engaging my students? Are audience response systems the answer to encouraging my students to share their ideas? How many activities should I include? Should I use Lego in my class to make my teaching more enjoyable? Whilst these are all valuable questions (and useful tools to employ as part of a 'teaching toolkit'), it seemed that these 'what works' style questions were the wrong ones to begin with. For me, these questions attended only to the surface of what might be taking place in the classroom.

I also agreed with Palmer that an excessive focus on technique was distracting the teachers I saw (including myself) from exploring some of the more significant questions. This meant that our actions and words appeared hollow, like the evocative image Palmer employs of the 'balloon speech in cartoons'. Instead, Palmer's call to attend to relationships, connections and integrity, his call to look *inside* as opposed to outside for a generic (meaningless) 'best' practice – felt radical and fresh, despite its publication date. Since then, I have played with similar ideas of my own regarding connections and integrity in the classroom for some years now, and one specific idea I have found powerful is the concept of vulnerability.

In particular, I have been interested in considering the question: what might the purpose and value be of sharing our own vulnerabilities as teachers in the classroom, in order to weave the 'web of connectedness' Palmer discusses? As Palmer suggests, the notion of expressing vulnerability is closely intertwined with how we perceive our roles and identities as teachers. Furthermore, it also knots and weaves with the role of power in the classroom. By sharing our own vulnerabilities, challenges and identities, we present ourselves as fallible and as ongoing learners, alongside our students. This disrupts the 'balloon speech' of a performative teacher and creates openings to potentially disrupt traditional teacher–student binaries and power hierarchies. However, this is not an easy thing for teachers to do. There is also an important question regarding how teachers can realistically practice vulnerability within the cultures of performativity and measurability that dominate contemporary higher education (and that we have explored in Chapter 2). With teachers' behaviours and credibility routinely scrutinized via measures such as module evaluation questionnaires, what spaces are available for teachers to take risks, and to express uncertainties, in front of the class? Is Palmer's teaching philosophy too idealistic for a twenty-first-century classroom?

Vulnerability in the Literature

These are questions and challenges that this chapter will explore, through a series of case studies with teachers, from the literature and from practice. Indeed, it is not just me who is interested in this idea. The value of teachers using vulnerability as a means to connect with learners and to develop relationships has surfaced in recent times as a key pedagogical question for teachers to consider. In their related articles, Elizabeth Molloy and Margaret Bearman (2017; 2018) offer the interesting concept of 'intellectual candour', or 'intellectual streaking', explaining this as the 'exposure of learners and teachers' thought processes, dilemmas or failures', as a way to make oneself vulnerable in the classroom in order to engage learners (2018: 32). Specifically, Molloy and Bearman examine how teachers might balance the tension between credibility and vulnerability, contending that the 'endemic need to promote credibility and hide vulnerabilities can, we argue, interfere with learning and quality of practice' (2018: 32).

Likewise, Daniela Mangione and Lin Norton (2020: 12) champion the role of vulnerability within teaching as a means to foster engagement. Mangione and Norton explore how vulnerability in teaching implies embracing uncertainty through collaboration and partnership. Mangione and Norton also consider the relationship of vulnerability and uncertainty to a marketized, metricized, sector, suggesting that vulnerability 'reinforces the values of higher education that go beyond the metrics and the employability market and seeks to engage students in deep transformative learning processes for a future that is uncertain and unknowable'. Harriet Schwartz (2019) and Stephen Brookfield (2015) have also both explored ideas of vulnerability as a means to foster connections, and as a route to disrupting power hierarchies, in their work. Building on these ideas, I examine specific instances of teacher vulnerability in the classroom and consider the practical ways to play with this concept. In particular, I consider its utility as a means to develop connections and relationships; however, I also consider some of the ongoing difficulties associated with vulnerability and candour in the classroom.

How does stepping off the stage, and being less of a sage, foster engagement? In a powerful extract drawing upon his teaching, Brookfield (2015: 4) explores how the sharing of his own anxieties regarding group discussion enabled his students to contribute:

An example of stumbling blindly into something approaching an appropriate response happened to me one day when I had prepared a series of dazzlingly provocative questions for discussion that I felt were bound to generate heated, rich, and informed conversation. I asked the first question and was met with blank stares and total silence. After counting off 15 seconds quietly in my head I then asked the follow-up question I had prepared. Again, silence. Now I started to panic and found myself answering the question I'd just asked. ... Dreadful, shaming quiet met my question along with the sound of my own blood rushing in my ears ...

With no forethought I found myself saying something like this: I know that speaking in discussions is a nerve-wracking thing and that your fear of making public fools of yourselves can inhibit you to the point of nonparticipation. I, myself, feel very nervous as a discussion participant and spend a lot of my time carefully rehearsing my contributions so as not to look foolish when I finally speak. So please don't feel that you have to speak in order to gain my approval or to show me that you're a diligent student. ... When anyone feels like saying something, just speak up. And if no-one does, then we'll move on to something else.

We can see that, through this sharing of vulnerabilities, Brookfield is working on a number of levels to break down barriers between himself and his students. These are barriers which the majority of teachers will no doubt have experiences of during their careers, with many of us having experienced the 'dreadful shaming quiet' Brookfield so aptly describes. Firstly, Brookfield voluntarily relinquishes some of his power as teacher, in order to show that he is a fallible human who finds situations difficult, like all of us, which is powerful to hear. Secondly, he demonstrates empathy and understanding to his students through sharing his own experiences of feeling nervous during class discussions. Thirdly, he shows his commitment to his students' learning, through his willingness to display such bravery and openness, and to articulate the problem. And then, he also demonstrates his own uncertainty and continued learning alongside his students. Brookfield admits that he does not know what will happen at all and is as uncertain along with the class. Brookfield continues to explain how, this admission 'seemed to unleash the conversational floodgates and a veritable torrent of student comment (well, it seemed like a torrent after the dry spigot of student silence) burst forth' (2015: 4). Beneath a seemingly innocuous statement of shared understanding, Brookfield was able to create a new space for his students to connect. On a further, and no less significant level, as an author, Brookfield is also sharing his vulnerabilities with us, his readers. In a myriad of ways, then, sharing our own challenges can be a powerful tool for those moments when we want to connect with our audience.

Similarly, in this extract below, Schwartz (2019: 86–7) explores what happened when she admitted she had made a mistake one day in class. Schwarz became aware that she had omitted to recognize the different experiences of students from different cultures, taking her own experience as universal, and assuming that all students felt similarly on a particular issue of discussion. The issue was attitudes to older people in society, and Schwarz had used the words 'our culture' to describe how older people are not commonly held in high esteem within societies. However, after an African American student pointed out her quite different perspective, Schwartz writes about how this incident forced her to acknowledge the limits to her own thinking:

> To admit I had made such an error felt vulnerable … However I was also aware that one of my deepest hopes for students in this class is that they will recognize, acknowledge, and seek to grow when their assumptions are inaccurate, that they will allow their worldview to expand, rather than hold on to the safety of surety. So the best use of my power in this moment was not to hide my realization and continue, but rather to admit my shortcoming.
>
> The vulnerability in the earlier exchange was revealing that I am still learning, and I still have blind spots in my world view. I am not suggesting we always go to a vulnerable place in front of the class. However, when I can appropriately reveal my imperfections, I hope I model for students that we can explore the inherent limitations of our world-views without shame. When we can be imperfect, admit our blind spots, ask difficult questions and reveal we do not understand, the learning space is expanded … The dominant cultural understanding of power brings to mind a dynamic that is rigid, closed and distant. Conversely power-with is dynamic … Perhaps we find power in vulnerability and in listening and responding to the other when we see power not as a zero-sum game.

As with Brookfield's experience, Schwartz's open acknowledgement of her mistake operates in a multiple of ways to enable her to connect to her class. Through demonstrating her own imperfections, she is able to role model the kind of growth she in turn expects from her students: presenting 'it as an essential step in the kind of growth we seek in the course'. She shares that she too is an ongoing learner, and that there is no shame in making mistakes so long as these are acknowledged. This enables her to metaphorically 'expand' the learning space and moves the dynamic from being 'rigid, closed and distant' towards a sharing of power, a 'power-with'.

Vulnerability in Practice

Inspired by these ideas, I explored how sharing my own vulnerabilities might work in the classroom. One particular example occurred during the teaching of a session for new lecturers and researchers on assessment and feedback approaches, as part of our Graduate Certificate in Learning and Teaching in Higher Education programme. My goal in this Continuing Professional Development workshop was to discuss with participants the emotional and affective impact of critical feedback upon the recipient, and to consider strategies that educators might employ to mitigate this impact, and that learners might employ to manage their own response. In doing so, I decided to share (anonymously) some examples of my own feedback I had received on my work, via anonymous peer review, when I first began writing articles for publication.

The comments I shared were the following:

Obviously, the paper is not based on a well-formulated research question.

It seemed to me as if they don't really understand what they are doing as researchers – as if they are going through the motions.

Another issue is the paragraph on reflexivity: I honestly couldn't figure out what the authors were trying to say here and why.

Because I initially share these comments anonymously, the class usually engages in a light-hearted debate about the harshness of the feedback and its likely impact upon the author. We usually laugh together about the tone of the comments, as well as their potential lack of use in offering a constructive pathway to improve. One reviewer writes unhelpfully: 'It seems to me that they don't really understand what they are doing.' And yet, no information as to how a greater level of understanding might be developed was forthcoming! As an exercise this works well in itself, however, it is when I reveal that these are comments that I received on my own work that I find that the atmosphere in the room usually changes. At this point, the learners often engage even further with both me and the exercise, commiserating or laughing with me at the experience. Students often feedback just how valuable they find this as an exercise. They report how realizing that a person who they perceive to be an experienced academic, and who has published a large body of work, also experiences critical and negative feedback is powerful.

They particularly seem to benefit from my openness in being willing to share my 'imperfections' with them, and the commitment I am demonstrating to their learning in doing so. The next step is usually a meaningful discussion about how I/we would respond to such feedback including employing strategies to manage the affective impact or to return to the work in progress. Whenever I do this exercise, I cannot help but think that the sharing of my own, quite embarrassing, experiences enables students to connect with both the topic of discussion as well as me, the teacher, on a powerful level.

After discussing some of these ideas with my colleagues in our department, we reflected upon the tension between sharing our vulnerabilities and the challenges of being presented as a polished, credible, academic. The following comment is from my colleague Naomi Winstone, a Professor in Educational Psychology:

> In academic circles, we typically only see the final polished articles produced by our colleagues; rarely do we have insight into the journey that they have taken to get to the point of publication. This insight has influenced my work as an academic developer, by encouraging me to share my own vulnerabilities and 'failures' in the classroom. I believe that sharing our own failures and how we have overcome them is more transformative for the academics with whom we work than examples of 'best practice'.

Naomi describes how sharing vulnerabilities is a crucial aspect of role modelling to others. Through role modelling we can use our experience to show others how we have learned to cope with challenging issues, for example receiving critical feedback. However, we can also use role modelling to foster connections and engagement, or to establish expectations and create a tone for the group's behaviour, as via the examples from Brookfield and Schwarz. As Bearman and Molloy (2017: 1284) argue, intellectual streaking or candour is 'the nimble exposure of a teacher's thought processes, dilemmas, or failures – as a way of modeling both reflection-in-action and resilience'. They write: 'We believe that there is value in the exposure of teachers' inner mechanisms to a wider, public audience. When we show our vulnerabilities, we illustrate that working within constraints and uncertainties are part of expert practice' (1284).

Thinking about our vulnerabilities as teachers and students may become even more valuable as a result of the Covid pandemic and the move to increased online or hybrid learning. For many teachers in higher education, the rapid 'pivot' to emergency remote teaching has been a considerable source of disruption. In the following extract, another colleague, Simon Lygo-Baker, a Senior Lecturer in higher education, explores his experience of vulnerability in the classroom, as a result of the move to remote online learning:

> For me, teaching has always been a challenge of exposure. This vulnerability is wrapped in different layers. I feel it because teaching involves a political dimension: as a teacher entering a classroom I take a position. Whatever stance I take, I will always remain vulnerable. The art of teaching for me relates to the constant decision making, often without any firm grounds or certainty, drawn from instinct, intuition or hope. The challenge has been to adapt, to find ways of exposing the vulnerability as constructive energy.
>
> The move to almost constant online teaching disrupted the vulnerability because the frames through which I was familiar no longer existed. The political dimension changed, I was, and remain, even less certain of what I do as a teacher and the link to learning. It has become an art form portrayed through a medium I am even less familiar. Like an artist forced to move from building layers through watercolour, now faced with having acrylic paint only. The landscape is familiar and yet unfamiliar. I know that I need to remain open to the exposure so that it can enact my integrity and yet it seems somehow more out of reach and abstract.

Here, Simon explains how vulnerability has always been important to his thinking and teaching. Importantly, vulnerability is both a 'challenge of exposure' and a 'constructive energy'. And yet, the move to 'almost constant online teaching' felt for him like an artist forced to change to an unfamiliar medium, raising new questions of uncertainty and vulnerability and of how to share this with his learners. We can see that vulnerability as a concept also offers a route to role modelling our own uncertainties and how we might respond to these, our own strategies for learning, coping or adapting to the unfamiliar. Just like our students, we are also learning, as exposed clearly via the example of teachers' move to teaching online: like unexpectedly being forced to paint with acrylics.

Potential Challenges and Complexities: Vulnerability in Situated Contexts

We can see from the examples above that the sharing of vulnerabilities has the potential to disrupt power binaries between teachers and students in radical ways. As a result, Molloy and Bearman suggest that teachers go first. When those with high social capital are prepared to open themselves to learning, and the concomitant possibility of loss, it creates an atmosphere of humility and possibility. Students may get a glimpse of the notion that they are on the same team as the teacher. (2018: 36)

However, relinquishing control and sharing power is not straightforward. It may not be as simple to express vulnerabilities, and to share 'social capital' in the classroom as it might appear. In this extract, Palmer considers how telling the truth in the workplace is an enterprise fraught with danger:

But telling the truth about ourselves with colleagues in the workplace is an enterprise fraught with danger, against which we have erected formidable taboos. We fear making ourselves vulnerable in the midst of competitive people and politics that could easily turn against us, and we claim the inalienable right to separate the 'personal' and the 'professional' into airtight compartments (even though everyone knows the two are inseparably intertwined). So we keep the workplace conversation objective and external, finding it safer to talk about technique than about selfhood. (1999: 119)

Palmer describes how the (artificially) binary construct of the personal and professional, separated into 'airtight compartments', offers teachers a shield in which they avoid talking about selfhood, and instead focus upon technique. This may be necessary, as teachers operate 'in the midst of competitive people and politics' that may easily 'turn against us'. How much are the competitive people and politics Palmer describes a barrier to expressing vulnerability, and to making connections with students?

Similarly, Edward Brantmeier (2013: 2) examines the tangled cultural, social and power dynamics that underpin an ostensibly simple concept:

The concept is simple – open yourself, contextualize that self in societal constructs and systems, co-learn, admit you do not know, and be human. Such simple statement might connate a sense of naiveté, however, in practice, the complex terrain of pedagogy of vulnerability is tangled given the power dynamics inherent in student and teacher cultural role sets. The burden of knowing the right answers, as expected by our students, bears tremendous weight. Simply understood, pedagogy of vulnerability is about taking risks – risks of self disclosure, risks of change, risks of not knowing, risks of failing – to deepen learning. Vulnerability is an act of courage. (2013: 2)

So, a pedagogy of vulnerability is a dangerous enterprise, and one that involves taking risks. And yet the key issue is that those risks are not experienced at the same level for all teachers. In the following extract, Brookfield (2017: 27) explores how learning interactions, and vulnerability, may be problematized by the identities of the student and teacher:

> Teacher and student identities outside the classroom also complicate life within it. In predominantly white institutions white teachers are given more credibility than teachers of color. As an older white male I can admit to mistakes with little fear of consequences. Indeed, my owning up to errors is usually read as a sign of endearing vulnerability: 'how courageous of you to share your foibles and mistakes with us!' Colleagues of color and female colleagues are much more likely to have their missteps interpreted as affirmative action giving jobs to incompetent and unqualified minorities. (2017: 27)

Here, Brookfield exposes the conflicting experience of students' responses to a white male's 'endearing vulnerability', against colleagues of different ethnicities or female teachers who may be interpreted as less competent, and whose credibility may be questioned when they seek to express vulnerability. We know that teachers are not perceived in the same ways, and do not exist independently from their racialized, classed and gendered bodies. Indeed, empirical research (Heffernan 2021) has surfaced the pervasive inequities in students' evaluations of teachers, revealing that student evaluations are influenced by racist, sexist and homophobic prejudices, and are biased against discipline and subject area.

Material actors also shape the learning and teaching relationship. These might be the student evaluations learners complete that directly feed into teachers' ability to be promoted or to retain their job, or it might be wider policy actors, for example, policy literature such as the UK Professional Standards Framework that creates expectations of teachers' continued progression towards certain benchmarks and standards of expertise. Similarly, the increasing value placed upon awards within the sector, for example, Advance HE's National Teaching Fellowship scheme, can also be seen to shape expectations of teacher behaviours. Advance HE explain that 'Achieving a National Teaching Fellowship is widely recognised in higher education within the UK as well as internationally as a mark of quality'. This is just one example of the increasing attention paid within the sector to the importance of measurable 'expertise'. Such expertise, accountability and quality standards may be experienced as at odds with teachers' ability to express uncertainties, vulnerabilities or to experiment within the classroom.

Moreover, as we saw from the comments by Simon Lygo-Baker, the Covid pandemic has raised new questions regarding teacher vulnerability, following the move to online and hybrid teaching. In addition, teaching in masks, to masked learners, in socially distanced classroom, raised new challenges for us to grapple with about interaction, and encouraged us to consider our identities and relationships as teachers in new ways. Similarly, the increased teacher visibility of online learning, with its inclusion of the presenter's face as a permanent mirror in the Zoom or Teams room, its exposure of our bedrooms, studies, kitchens, children and pets, or with its requirement for recorded content to be made available online, all leads to important ethical and pedagogical questions surrounding teacher visibility and vulnerability. Likewise, new questions arise regarding students' visibility when learning online. Students may express their vulnerabilities by choosing to turn their cameras off and remain private. This option may not be afforded to teachers, and teaching content may be vulnerable to being repurposed or misused from online sources. These ideas are explored further in work by Sian Bayne and colleagues, for example, in their Manifesto of Teaching Online (2020), where the authors examine the risks of surveillance cultures in relation to online teaching and learning, and consider the ongoing issues pertaining to teacher visibility in the digital university.

Despite their best efforts, then, educators may experience that pedagogies of openness and vulnerability sit uncomfortably with traditional student and institutional expectations of teacher expertise, or with the challenges and affordances of new post-Covid teaching environments, and that these expectations are expressed through a breadth of sociomaterial actors, and intertwined in complex and durable ways with social relations, and inequalities. In many contexts, as Molloy and Bearman identify, there may be a need for teachers to maintain credibility.

> A first-year medical student can be expected to ask silly questions; a new consultant has to strive harder to appear expert. A well-respected senior clinician with a prolific research profile may feel very comfortable in replying to a delegate at a conference with: 'That is a very good question. I don't have the answer to that.' The attribution of credibility affords different social responses with different effects. We particularly suggest that teachers can use intellectual candour to promote student learning. This is not risk-free. Although humility is a very appealing attribute in someone of high status and 'making oneself vulnerable' can also boost credibility as well as diminish it, there is always a potential fall in credibility. (2018: 35)

Humility is an 'appealing attribute' but it comes at a cost. This cost is one that may not be affordable for some teachers working in higher education today. As Mangione and Norton (2020: 1–2) explain, a tension exists between the discourses of higher education that are dominated by an attention to metrics and marketization: 'The call for control and accountability has put the emphasis on a metrics-driven approach to quality and a narrow conception of teaching excellence.' This culture can be constraining for teachers who may want to explore conceptions of vulnerability, and explore their own identities within the classroom, in order to foster authentic relationships with their students founded on trust. Rather, these constraints and the pressures of accountability may create the likelihood that teachers teach defensively and safely (Kinchin and Winstone 2017).

Some disciplines may also offer less fertile ground for teachers to express vulnerabilities, particularly those disciplines where the pursuit of an objective truth is considered a valid goal. Similarly, some students may be less comfortable relinquishing their trust placed in their teachers. This may be more commonly the case within certain cultures, for example, cultures who may have more hierarchical student–teacher relations embedded in societal norms. Teaching is therefore both a sociomaterial and situated practice that cannot be understood as divorced from its social, material, political, historical and cultural contexts. And yet, too often the literature and practice is dominated by a cognitive psychological framing, described powerfully by Catherine Manathunga as a focus on individuals 'and on their brains as separate from their raced, classed, gendered bodies and the social, historical, political and cultural contexts within which they learn' (2011: 355). There are a number of inherent ethical risks with evaluating individuals as divorced from their bodies and contexts, meaning that notions of pedagogy too often become 'bleached of their complexity and richness … and reduced to narrow, technical "professional rules for practice"' (2011: 356). There can be no blanket rules for practice, and there also needs to be a much greater understanding of the granular, situated day-to-day experiences of teachers.

Indeed, a further challenge to vulnerability might be its widespread adoption as a 'practice' at all. Arguably, vulnerability is not something teachers should perform. And yet 'faux vulnerability' is already a known problem within teaching and learning. For example, Bruce Macfarlane and Lesley Gourlay (2009) discuss how the reflective assignment, so widely used in teacher education, fosters a culture akin to the reality TV show. Within this culture, students are expected to share how they have overcome their challenges, to share their transformative journeys, and to follow prescribed paths of self-disclosure and discovery. For Macfarlane and Gourlay (2009: 458) the forced enactment of these vulnerabilities and learning journeys can result in 'a grotesque simulacrum of authenticity'. Students and teachers espousing formulaic narratives of self-discovery, and performing practices of 'faux vulnerability', would be about as far away from Palmer's call to consider our own integrity and identity as possible. Such inauthenticity is something that we should be mindful of and that should be guarded against.

Similarly, another potential challenge is that such a focus on teachers' identities may shift the gaze entirely onto what teachers do, or worse *must* do, to foster meaningful learning interactions. Macfarlane and Gourlay describe how the twin ideologies of teacher-centred and student-centred approaches to learning have created their own set of dogmas (2009: 458). Connections are not about centring learning with teachers, students – or indeed anywhere. Rather, learning might be more usefully understood as an interconnected, rhizomatic web of relations that includes a multiple of actors. Vulnerability is about creating a space for openness and connections within the web. Students also have a responsibility to engage and if they do not then the teacher should not feel like they have failed. Arguably, there should always be an element of shared responsibility, a partnership, in effective teaching, and concepts of partnership and co-creation are ideas that I explore further in Chapter 5.

Conclusion

The concept of vulnerability is one that I and other teachers have found useful as part of a range of ideas that can be explored and played with in order to foster connections with learners in the classroom. In this chapter, I have explored some practical examples of how teachers have drawn upon their own identities and integrity in the classroom in order to disrupt traditional teacher–student hierarchies, to foster more generative and dialogic relationships, and to share our own uncertainties with our learners. Accepting our vulnerabilities and discussing our own challenges openly can lead to a new kind of culture, one in which failures and mistakes are more readily accepted and perfectionism and competition is less dominant. Through creating more open dialogic and collaborative cultures we may take valuable steps towards making students feel like they matter.

However, I also suggest that generalizable rules for practice are not helpful, and that any consideration of practical strategies for engagement should be understood within the situated contexts in which learning and teaching occurs. Sociomaterial theorists, such as Tara Fenwick, Richard Edwards and Peter Sawchuk (2011), have shown that teaching and learning does not exist in a vacuum, and that learning is produced relationally amongst teacher, learners and the environment, as opposed to being dependent on a teacher's essential self. Newer teachers, teachers on precarious contracts, female teachers, teachers feeling estranged within predominantly white spaces or teachers who are constrained by the forces of metricization and measurement for whatever reason, may not be able to take the risks that I and other colleagues have discussed here. There is also an urgent need for student evaluations of teaching to acknowledge the differentiated treatment of teachers and the inherent biases and prejudices that play out in the classroom. Further, the teaching environments we find ourselves in following the Covid pandemic, and within the contemporary digital university, have raised new ethical and pedagogical questions for teachers regarding visibility, vulnerability and interaction. Teaching practice should be tailored to the individual, to the individual's identity and values and to the learning environment. Teachers may need to develop their own personal philosophy of teaching, whilst also attending to the wider impact of such a philosophy, that recognizes the role of the teacher as part of a wider whole. Indeed, this may be a new and generative way of understanding the contested concept of teaching excellence which acknowledges the relationality and fluidity of our practice (Gravett and Kinchin 2020). While it may be useful to suggest ideas to try, we should also remain mindful that nothing works for all teachers in all situations; teaching is always messy, uncertain and situated. In Chapter 4, I continue to consider ideas surrounding how teachers can explore their own identities, and can develop meaningful connections with students. In doing so, I focus on the complex concept of authenticity and its utility for thinking about student–teacher relationships.

4

Authenticity and Trust in Teaching and Learning

Introduction

In this chapter, I explore the role of two related concepts, authenticity and trust, considering how these ideas might be useful in fostering meaningful connections between teachers and students. What value might they be for thinking about higher education, and how might they be important within relational pedagogies? Students often report that the most significant aspect of their relationships with tutors is their feeling that the tutor genuinely cares, that they matter to that teacher and that this connection is authentic. However, authenticity has been shown to be a complex and elusive concept, and poststructural and posthuman scholarship has radically destabilized uniform and singular interpretations of the self, and of meaning. If relations and actions can be interpreted in a number of different ways, and if there are multiple ways of knowing, being and doing, do ideas of authenticity and trust still have any value within an understanding of relational pedagogies? I will consider what these concepts might mean for teachers' relationships with students, and what role they might play in a contemporary understanding of pedagogies of mattering.

In order to do this, I will draw upon the literature, upon recent research, and upon critical conversations with other educators. In particular, I draw upon a specific conversation with a teacher whose work has greatly inspired my own teaching and so many others in the field: Professor Stephen Brookfield. Brookfield has written extensively on a breadth of issues affecting pedagogy and society, including how teachers can employ the values of credibility or authenticity, how they can use vulnerability and role modelling to develop trust and how they might attend to and surface power relations in the classroom. These are predominant themes that have been addressed over many years in the higher education literature, but which, arguably, take on greater resonance as teachers experience new pressures within increasingly complex contexts, as explored in Chapters 2 and 3. In the following chapter, I consider how the concepts of authenticity and trust have been treated more broadly in the education literature, and what this might mean for how we can use them in our work. Stephen Brookfield and I then explore the resonance of the ideas of authenticity, trust and mattering further, via a critical conversation.

Theorizing authenticity, Trust and Mattering in Higher Education

What is authenticity and why might it be a useful idea for thinking about learning? In a study with undergraduate student participants (Gravett and Winstone 2020), who were asked to write stories and to attend interviews in order to discuss their experiences of university life, my colleague Naomi Winstone and I explored the importance of connections in student and staff relationships. Our findings suggested that there is a clear need to foreground the value of meaningful relationships and relational pedagogies within higher education and where possible to push back upon neoliberal practices that may obstruct academics' ability to meaningfully connect with their students (2020). Students spoke of their need to feel that their tutors genuinely cared about them as individuals and that this genuine interaction led to a feeling of authenticity that went beyond textbook approaches to teaching. Karen Barad argues that every intra-action matters (2007). This idea of intra-action (as opposed to interaction) evokes the idea of the connected nature of relationships and Barad suggests that every relational connection is significant. The importance of authenticity as a concept in teaching has also been examined in the work of Nel Noddings (1986). Noddings employs the concept of relational 'fidelity', which encourages us to consider the authenticity of relational interactions and she suggests that the use of fidelity – understood as focusing on the individual and the quality of that relationship with an individual – can offer an underpinning value for teachers. Likewise, Harriet Schwarz (2019) argues that authenticity is intertwined with the notion of mattering:

> When I think back to my most important teachers and mentors, I realise that feeling as if I mattered to them was a common thread in all the relationships what I found compelling was a sense that I was not just another student passing through but that they saw me and recognised my aspirations and potential.

Authenticity is essential. Only when we are authentic will students trust our words, and this trustworthiness gives expressions of mattering their credence and value ... When we convey to students their thinking matters and their ideas have influenced or inspired us we reduce the hierarchy in the relationship. (131–9)

There are a lot of interesting ideas here. For Schwarz, authenticity is about awareness: an awareness of ourselves, our students as well as the wider context. Authenticity and trust can enable teachers to convey mattering, and this can then help to reduce power hierarchies. Crucially, mattering enables students to feel as though they are 'not just another student passing through'. Similarly, in the work by Katherine Wimpenny and Maggi Savin-Baden (2013) which synthesizes the research literature and explores alienation, agency and authenticity in relation to student engagement, the authors conclude that

> consistently, the importance of tutors adequately conveying genuineness and empathic understanding to student learning, acknowledging students' struggles, and insecurities, pleasures and pains was expressed. Tutors need to support students in recognising the ways in which aspects of their lives impact upon engagement in pedagogic spaces. (324)

Caroline Kreber and colleagues have also explored how authenticity might be useful to our understanding of learning and teaching (Kreber et al. 2007; Kreber 2010). Kreber argues that personal conceptions of teaching interact with authenticity in a sense that 'our conceptions of learners should be compatible with caring for students ... and engaging students in dialogue around issues that matter' (2010: 90). Kreber suggests that pedagogies that are authentic can be understood 'in the wider sense that the student's being is engaged in the teaching–learning interaction' (2010: 191). Similar ideas have also been explored by Akram Ramezanzadeh and colleagues (2017: 299) who conceptualize authenticity as a 'deep understanding of pedagogical relationships, critical reflection, and self-reflection,' and as involving 'the constant process of becoming that deepened [teachers'] understanding of themselves and others'. While Merlin Thompson (2015: 617) also offers a detailed analysis of authenticity and concludes that 'authenticity survives in the messy interplay of self-understanding, self-care, and self-acceptance'.

The concepts of authenticity, and of an authentic learning community, also pervade the work of Parker Palmer (1998, 1999) who explores ideas of identity, integrity and selfhood in his work. Palmer's evocative image of the balloon speech in cartoons to describe the feeling learners experience when teachers play-act the role of teacher, following textbook, or rote approaches or techniques, memorably depicts how inauthenticity can be perceived by students (1998: 67). Specifically, Palmer also explores notions of relational trust: 'relational trust is built on movements of the human heart such as empathy, commitment, compassion, patience and the capacity to forgive' (1998: xvii). For Palmer, this all forms part of the 'inner work' (1998: xvii) of a teacher: trust, mattering and connectedness is at the heart of authentic education.

Who Is the We That Matters?

However, there are a number of complexities relating to how we might understand human connections. Sociological critiques of individuality (e.g. Giddens 1991; Bauman 2000) have problematized ideas of a coherent self – for example, Giddens, who explains how 'the biography the individual reflexively holds in mind is only one "story" among many other potential stories that could be told about her development as a self' (1991: 9). For Giddens, 'the reflexive project of the self generates programmes of actualisation and mastery'; and yet, authenticity might be a pre-eminent value and a framework for self-actualization, but it actually represents 'a morally stunted process' (1991: 9). Poststructural thinkers and Indigenous and feminist scholars have also argued that there may be many stories told about one particular event, and that meaning is multiple and open to a plurality of interpretations. Likewise, Katherine Wimpenny and Maggi Savin-Baden (2013: 323–4) highlight the complexity and multiplicity of student engagement with higher education, and argue that engagement with learning is ultimately a subjective experience. Such ideas problematize the notion of any authentic interaction.

A central assumption within many Western cultures is that a person has a true identity or core self that can be actualized. Yet the concept of a core self that is fixed and enduring also sits uncomfortably with contemporary understandings of the self as changing and developing, in a state of 'becoming' (Deleuze and Guattari 1987; Gravett 2021). Similarly, the sociologist Daniel Miller (2010: 17–19) writes that

> in both philosophy and everyday life we imagine that there is a real or true self which lies deep within us … It is as though if we peeled off the outer layers we would finally get to the real self within. Actually … we are all onions. If you keep peeling off our layers you find – absolutely nothing left. There is no true

inner self ... Deep inside ourselves is blood and bile, not philosophical certainty. (2010: 17–19)

How to reconcile the notion of authenticity in learning and teaching with self as onion? Brookfield has also troubled straightforward concepts of authenticity, explaining how hierarchical cultures and differences in identities disrupt a teacher's commitment to authenticity and benevolent notions of 'at-one-ness':

> I assume that the sincerity with which I invest them is clear and that it produces the desired positive effects in students. I also assume that my actions designed to democratize the classroom, engage students, and convey authenticity are experienced in the way I intend. But ... I know that my assumption that declaring my at-one-ness with students causes them to see me as one of them is way too naive. In fact, the strongly hierarchical culture of higher education, with its structures of authority and its clear demarcation of roles and boundaries, means that I can't simply wish my influence away. No matter how much I might want it to be otherwise and no matter how informal, friendly, and sincere I might be in my declarations of at-one-ness, I am viewed as fundamentally different. (2017: 14)

Here, Brookfield explains that despite his sincere efforts to democratize the classroom, the culture of higher education, as a microcosm within society, means that roles and boundaries are already clearly demarcated and his influence and power cannot be easily reduced.

Much of the education literature has attended to issues of power in the classroom. In particular, the field has been heavily indebted to Michel Foucault's writings on power, particularly Foucault's depiction of power as situated outside of the individual, as well as his explorations of the pervasive and durable nature of power (1975, 1976). Carol Taylor and Carol Robinson (2009) also problematize dominant conceptions of power: as encompassing a lack of recognition of the implications of the gendered, raced and classed teacher, and as being underpinned by a modernist, rationalistic, universalist concept of the person. Exploring the challenges surrounding student voice work, Taylor and Robinson (2009) warn of other challenges that educators face in seeking to disrupt power relations in higher education, 'given the dominance of the performance-related, standards discourse, it is against this hegemonic discourse that any student voice work which has a genuinely transformative or radical potential might have to struggle to construct its practices' (2009: 167). Elizabeth Ellsworth (1989) also problematizes the notion of power and revisits key concepts including empowerment, and dialogue, provocatively describing these concepts as 'repressive myths'. Ellsworth (1989) explains that many of these fundamental concepts are more nuanced and more problematic than we might imagine:

> Acting as if our classroom were a safe space in which democratic dialogue was possible and happening did not make it so. Dialogue in its conventional sense is impossible in the culture at large because at this historical moment, power relations between raced, classed, and gendered students and teachers are unjust. (315)

For Ellsworth, power relations underscore learning and teaching interactions, and yet dialogic approaches are often recommended uncritically. Ellsworth (1989) contends that we need to unlearn key assumptions and assertions of current literature on critical pedagogy. These ideas remind us of being wary of simplistic, humanist approaches to understanding connections exposing that relationships are impacted upon by a much broader context, involving key actors such as power, space and a breadth of broader materialities. Relations are not simply social or discursive interactions that can be controlled by the humans involved: 'Acting as if our classroom were a safe space in which democratic dialogue was possible and happening did not make it so'. In the following section, I will use the critical conversation with Stephen Brookfield to further elaborate some of these ideas regarding power, authenticity and mattering.

A Critical Conversation

This conversation with Stephen Brookfield took place on 26 October 2020, online via Zoom, and was subsequently continued via email. In the dialogue that follows, we surface some of the key issues related to connections and mattering in learning and teaching, and unpack further Brookfield's values-based concept of pedagogy. Specifically, given that in the dominant discourses of higher education, narratives of resilience, expertise and measurable 'performance' are often espoused, we explore whether despite this there is still a place for a more relational, values-based, pedagogy, and what challenges might remain for teachers who wish to enact this.

Karen Gravett: I am wondering, Stephen, if you would be happy to share with us what you most enjoy about teaching?

Stephen Brookfield: What I enjoy is the interchange with students ... as a teacher my philosophy is whatever students say will be helpful to their learning that's where usually I will go first. But I mostly like the give and take of discussion and raising questions and listening carefully to what students are saying and asking a good question. I'm very proud of a good question, an open-ended question, that I myself don't really know the answer to, that's not been planned beforehand. I love when in the middle of a carefully prepared class I'll do a 180 degree turn because something has occurred to me. I find that very creatively fulfilling, I guess part of the joy is more student-centred seeing people making connections seeing someone who has not spoken in the term up to that point suddenly saying something – that's a big thrill to me. There's this selfish pleasure you get from in the moment doing something that you feel is right. It's a kind of pedagogic grace, that sounds a bit pretentious, but you know you just get this sense that this is really working … I think these are probably the greatest sources of joy.

Karen Gravett: You've touched upon how one of your values is being helpful. Can you expand on that and tell us how your values inform your teaching?

Stephen Brookfield: Well, I've always seen a sort of sociopolitical dimension to teaching, it's not just initiating someone into the grammar of the subject … One of the things I'm very intrigued with is student to student power, and also the power of a teacher. And whether you are ethical and responsible in your use of power or whether you are abusive and authoritarian. Critical theory is really useful in helping me to understand that and many, many, other things. I think part of that comes also from a belief in collectivism and the group and the value of collaboration. I have a suspicion of individual, overly individualistic, ways of learning and overly individualistic ways of testing, and individualistic ways of teaching. The best form of teaching to me which goes to this idea of collaboration and utility, is team teaching, because when students see team teaching properly conceived happening they see people asking each other questions, challenging each other, not trying to win each other over, but exercising curiosity, agreeing to disagree, living with that disagreement thinking through what that tension means for them. Thinking critically about each others' positions, asking each other good critical questions. And when we say we want students to think critically, which most people I think in higher education would say 'yeah I would like my students to think critically', there's very few models of that, for them for students. You know, I mean, I guess we can try and think critically in front of people ourselves, but it's much easier with one or two colleagues in the room who can bring up a different perspective. Ask you a really good question and point out an alternative view point or alternative framework, alternative perspective. Show that you're listening to each other, responding to each other. We don't have good models I think of active listening and responding the students can then adopt in discussion. So as you know, I've always felt strongly that modelling is very important from teachers and again the reason why I think its importance has to do with being useful, giving students a sense of, you know, this is what I am trying to do now. I'd like having done that to turn it over to you and ask you to, you know, engage in the same kind of activity.

Karen Gravett: Thank you. Yes, that was definitely going to be one of my questions in terms of the way that you often use role modelling as you say and also use a lot of autobiographical stories about in your teaching. And, even openly sharing emotive issues, for example racism and white supremacy, and so it seems like that openness and the use of story is a really important element of your teaching would you say?

Stephen Brookfield: Yeah it really is. I think that this is true for me and for a lot of other people. You can read very dense prose, you can listen to a beautifully crafted lecture, and there will be arguments maybe statistics and information and theories in there but the thing that will stick most strongly is if a story piece of narrative is used to illustrate an extremely complex argument. So, it's not storytelling for the sake of entertaining or storytelling. It's storytelling as a way of conveying complexity. And if you can encapsulate some idea, some contradiction, you are trying to get across in a personal story that's what really sticks with people. I began my teaching career studiously never saying anything personal. I began teaching in Lewisham in further education and students would ask me about my personal life. And I would say 'you know that's irrelevant'. And then over the years when I started playing around with in class assessment, getting immediate feedback from students on what was standing out from a particular in-class session, it was really clear that if, by accident, I had said something personal that's what everybody remembered. So I thought, well, and this was remarkably consistent across environments, so I thought, OK, if this is what's coming out from the data I'm collecting then I really need to take it seriously and work at integrating personal narrative and story and get over this sense that it's unprofessional for example to share something personal, so that really hit me I don't know about twenty years ago. I've been teaching fifty years. So it probably took me about thirty years to realize what I'd wished I'd known a lot earlier!

So, then, now I'm doing a lot of work which is extremely creatively challenging around race, like as you mentioned, and white supremacy. And so yes one of my credos is that I should never come in and pretend that I am the authoritative expert who is beyond racism. I should start off talking about what's happened to me today, yesterday, last week in terms of feeling some racist instincts and impulses and doing, you know I am committing some racial micro-aggressions, jokes, the way I direct my eye contact in a meeting, who I should call upon in class, the examples that I use, the texts that I automatically go to. I should start by giving personal examples of how I struggle with my own learned racism before I ask anybody else to talk about it. So, yeah, you're right the modelling and the autobiographical elements are really, again, axiomatic. I think they're foundational in the way I do think about teaching these days.

I think there's a danger with it though which is that sometimes if you start talking about yourself, people think 'Oh my god. Look at this guy who thinks he is so profound and so important that he has to share everything about himself with us!' So, it can backfire. It can be seen as, you know, self-obsession, self-indulgence. But usually, I keep a Backchannel chat (http://backchannelchat.com/), a social media thing open in every class and I check that about every 15 minutes and that will tell me the postings on there if I am going too far off track and I do feel if you use autobiographical information, actually with everything, you have to explain why you're doing it and justify why you're doing it. And one of the things I tell junior colleagues these days is you can, I think, you can never over explain why you are doing what you are doing making it clear and public to students the rationale informing your choice of activity, why you have designed this assignment the way you have and why you chose the texts or the videos that you chose for students to view and then in the middle of the class if you change your plan explain why you changed your plan. … And I think a lot of this also applied to the practice of leadership. Being willing to be as open and as transparent as possible. And just talking people why you're doing what you're doing – there's something in that that I think builds a level of trust.

Karen Gravett: Yes, because you've written about how the credibility and authenticity are perhaps the two most important characteristics of being an effective teacher, so I guess that's what you are really talking about here – authenticity and trust?

Stephen Brookfield: Yeah, I think trust. I mean the best experience I ever had as a student was doing a PhD at the University of Leicester. And unlike here in the States – this was true at least when I was a PhD student – I never had to take exams. I didn't take courses. You know I just convinced someone at the University that I had a good idea and he agreed to supervise me, and then we would just meet and talk, and then three years later I presented a thesis and graduated. But throughout that experience he would constantly create problems for me. And so, over the three years, he would put roadblocks in my way, but I never felt that the roadblocks were for the sake of derailing me. I always knew that the questions he was asking, the problems he was posing, were good for me in that they really moved me forward with my research and helped me understand what I was dealing with a bit better. So, I got really interested in why am I trusting this guy so much? Even though he's creating problems for me? And I thought it's because from the way he asked me questions, the way he conveys information, the way he explains himself, I know that he has my best interests at heart. He wants this to be a really good piece of work. And so I thought a lot about trust at that time and the use of power. Because of course a PhD supervisor has incredible life or death power over you and I thought he's using his power authority in a very empowering way. It's really helping me grow as a person and progress. So, I think ever since that time, which is a really long time ago, I've really been interested in trust and how that develops. And when I got into the whole project of helping people to think critically … I knew somehow that you can't do that unless there is trust. They have to have this sense that you're not just playing a game to catch them out or humiliate them they have to have the sense that you are doing it for good reasons and ultimately that this will be helpful to them … so trust is the thing that I've really tried to spend a lot of time understanding, and trust as the responsible use of power and authority is something that I have thought a lot about.

Karen Gravett: Thanks so much for sharing that. Definitely one of the most affecting areas of your work for me is when I started reading your writings about discussion. And how, alive beneath these seemingly neutral opportunities, power is there, but usually we think about discussion as naturally open, and generative, and positive, but the power is there and as you say it can be really stifling. I'm intrigued about how power is an important theme within your work. Can you talk a little but more about that?

Stephen Brookfield: Yes, it comes from my research into my own students, partly because when I read end-of-week evaluations of what happened in class if I've been using a lot of conversational approaches one of the most consistent themes, critical themes, will often be that too few people are dominating too much of the conversation, and sometimes if you have two really garrulous people in the class they can be responsible for 95 per cent of the discussion … But you can be completely disconnected from that so I do feel that we have to use our power to intervene, and to equalize and democratize participation as much as is possible … I think working in a democratic way means deliberately altering the sort of rhythms, the modalities, that you use in the classroom. So I will have large group discussion and invariably the large group discussion will probably be about 15 per cent who will talk but then I will stop and I will say 'you know I think this is helpful, there are some good points here, I know that it's often helpful for me to listen to how others are thinking this through as a way of coming to some understanding myself but now we're going to move into a different modality' … so I think you have to use your authority as a teacher to create environments as best you can where everybody does at some point have the chance to feel they're being noticed, they're being encouraged to contribute so that's a big interest of mine …

and I'm always intrigued in how students interpret my use of the power that I have. I think I spent a long time early in my career pretending that I didn't have any power. Wanting to be the students' friend, thinking if I wanted to work inclusively and democratically then I have to be the same as them. And then through experience and through reading Foucault's work, I understood that power is inevitable. And I do have power and authority and probably the best thing I can do is just acknowledge that and tell them the basis under which my authority is to be exercised. And then I read Paulo Freire and Ira Shor's conversation (1987) where they talk about the difference between being authoritative and being authoritarian. That was a real help to me, I've referred to that a lot. And I thought, yes, being authoritative is a completely different thing from being authoritarian and you can be, often with people, particularly if your work you're entering a new domain of learning where you feel uncertain and intimidated, you need the sense that you have an authoritative teacher who you can trust – again, trust – to lead you into this new domain. So I stopped pretending that I was no different from the students and started to acknowledge that, of course I had authority and, if I'm grading their work and deciding what kind of grade whether they pass the course it's incumbent on me to be very explicit about how I'm using that authority.

Karen Gravett: Can you tell us more about in your view how does a focus on the values of authenticity, and vulnerability, work in the context of increased pressures upon teachers to be accountable, strong/resilient, and consistent within the performative university?

Stephen Brookfield: Of course, stressing authenticity and vulnerability sit at odds with the development of metrics of measurable behaviours across different contexts. The forms that I've been assessed by have, over the years, stressed my ability to explain things clearly, to create opportunities for students to ask questions, how frequently I give feedback, whether I'm available in office hours and so on. These things are obviously important but there's a performative dimension to them. They can be measured in terms of frequency and public performance. But if a key dynamic in helping people think more critically is the degree to which my students trust me, how is a metric going to capture that? And how can I possibly be assessed as regards my trustworthiness, given that people come to a point of trust in multiple ways?

The contemporary emphasis on strength and resilience – on 'grit' – is very interesting to me, because modelling an openness and vulnerability is an act that requires great strength. Yet, that act is perceived very differently depending on questions of positionality and identity. If I admit to making a mistake, or if I talk about how I'm constantly being made aware of my own learned racism, I typically get plaudits. People congratulate me on my 'courage' and 'vulnerability'. Yet, when I've team taught with women and colleagues of colour, the exact same behaviour of going public with a vulnerable disclosure is often received very differently. If my female colleagues go public with any mistakes they've made, they are seen as incompetent or unprofessional. If my colleagues of colour do the same thing they risk being viewed by students as holding their positions only because of affirmative action. So although modelling vulnerability is important, we need to acknowledge how that behaviour is differentially perceived depending on the enactor's identity.

In the same way that mandatory reflective practice can be an instrument of control and surveillance (rather than an opportunity for surprise, exploration and growth), mandating and operationalizing vulnerability is something I would not want to see. If you start specifying standard vulnerable behaviours, then you underscore the most superficial aspects of performativity. You'll reduce teachers to checking off in their heads internalized injunctions to 'use a personal example' every fifteen minutes, or 'admit to at least two errors per lesson'. The fundamentally relational nature of teaching for critical thinking just can't be 'canned' in that way. How trust develops varies so much from person to person. It can't be standardized.

Karen Gravett: And finally, can you articulate further your conception of a pedagogy of grace and how this relates to the values you've discussed?

Stephen Brookfield: When I use the phrase 'pedagogy of grace' I mean being in a state of flow; a state of working spontaneously and responding in the moment to whatever's happening. It's not something you can plan for, so it can't be captured or measured in any kind of metric. It happens when you're responding 'on the fly' to a situation – maybe to a question that someone's raised – and you do something completely unprepared and unexpected that, in the moment you're doing it, feels completely *right*. This sense of appropriateness can't be put into words as it's taking place, though as you reflect back on what happened you can start to unearth some of the dynamics in play and perhaps understand what elements in your experience prompted you to act as you did. But at that moment you feel as if you're flying. It's immeasurably joyful and satisfying and represents an emotional highlight in your career. Once you've experienced a moment of profound joy like that you want to keep recreating it. But of course you can't. The grace comes from the moment's unpredictability.

This search for grace can be seductively dangerous. After all, there's no necessary correlation between you feeling satisfied and joyful, and what your students are learning. Your apparent moment of grace may be deeply confusing to students. You may believe your action or comment to be immensely creative and helpful, but that doesn't mean students feel the same about it. They might not understand what you're trying to do or say, or may miss your comment or action entirely! So one's personal experience of grace must always be checked against students' perceptions of what they found most helpful to their learning.

Concluding Thoughts

In this critical dialogue, we explored a number of key themes relating to teaching in higher education. Our conversation took place against the backdrop of a sector that has changed shape dramatically in recent years. In this conversation, we consider what concepts such as authenticity, power and trust might mean in the classroom, and how thinking critically about these ideas may offer potential for educators to think differently about learning and teaching. These ideas cannot resolve the myriad of challenges teachers in higher education experience. Indeed, we have considered how sincere attempts at authenticity, democracy and vulnerability may be complicated by power relations, hierarchical structures and inequities between staff and student identities. Our conversation closes with the consideration of the need to remain critical and thoughtful about our practice, and to continue dialogues with students in order to understand how teaching and learning may be experienced.

While we have seen that concepts of authenticity and trust can be useful in enabling educators to think about their responsiveness to their students, and how they offer ideas that can speak back to performative, metrics-based conceptions of how teachers and students might experience higher education, we have also seen how complex relationships are, and how they are shaped by identity, positionality and broader non-human factors such as power and space. We might conclude that key to authenticity is the idea of responsiveness, which includes attempting to listen to and know the individual, fully attending and engaging with the individual and also developing trust. We might not be able to (or want to) develop a fixed, authentic self, but we can work towards authentic interactions, underscored where possible by care, trust and responsiveness. As Brookfield explains when describing his meaningful connection with his supervisor: 'from the way he asked me questions, the way he conveys information, the way he explains himself, I know that he has my best interests at heart'.

However, interactions have been shown to be even more complex than we might have assumed following the Covid-19 pandemic. In Covid and post-Covid assemblages, small things matter: a Zoom room, a sign, a mask, headphones all possess 'thing power' (Bennett 2009) and shape the learning and teaching environment in new ways. The pandemic has brought into focus the fundamental role of non-human actors within our working and learning lives. How might the ideas of authenticity and trust fit within a post-Covid assemblage? Connections may feel more difficult to establish remotely, or through socially distanced, masked teaching. Learners and teachers may be preoccupied by the myriad of anxieties raised by the pandemic, or with issues of increased visibility and surveillance as explored in Chapter 3. Unstable technological connections and poor equipment not designed for hybrid interactions may obstruct meaningful interactions. But pre-Covid too, poorly designed classrooms, large class sizes where not all students can be seated, and the material pressures of a precarious workforce, who may be simply too busy to get to know their students, all impact on how authenticity and trust might be fostered in higher education.

In response to some of these challenges, Carol Taylor suggests that we might adopt a situated, moment-to-moment approach:

> Every pedagogic practice or research instance [might] be reconceptualised as an ongoing delicate and necessary engagement with a 'we' made anew moment by moment. All this rightly calls attention to, and radically complicates, any easy assumptions about who 'we' are, who 'we' can become who we can/should. might want to speak for, and who we include/are including when we use the word we ethical relationality involves understanding how our different experiences and histories position us in relation to one another. (2019: 18)

This complexity resonates with the ideas discussed in this chapter and specifically with Brookfield's description of a pedagogy of grace: 'This selfish pleasure you get from in the moment doing something that you feel is right. It's a kind of pedagogic grace ... you just get this sense that this is really working ... I think these are probably the greatest sources of joy.' Perhaps in order to generate authentic connections and trust, we need to accept the complexity of our engagements with one another, the multiple interpretations, and the challenges and differences that meaningful relationships generate. But we can perhaps also remain hopeful; as bell hooks suggests, 'The classroom with all its limitations remains a location of possibility' (1994: 207).

5

Student–Staff Partnerships as Relational Practice

Introduction

In the last chapter within this section that attends to teachers' relationships with students, I explore the area of student–staff partnerships, or co-creation. I examine what student–staff partnerships might offer as a means to disrupt power relations, to create new openings for connections, and to think differently about relationships within teaching and learning. How does working in partnership with students make students and teachers feel? What changes can happen as a result of student–staff partnerships, in terms of how we think about key concepts such as power, agency, connections and mattering? This chapter will feature data drawn from interviews with staff and students who have engaged in partnership activities, in order to draw upon a rich breadth of voices, and to offer diverse perspectives on what student–staff partnerships might have to offer educators in higher education. However, I will also consider what might be the challenges to working in more affirmative and relational ways. How might we enact authentic student–staff partnerships in higher education, and avoid partnership being adopted instrumentally by institutions – becoming the tokenistic 'ventriloquism' described by Bruce Macfarlane (2016). How can we ensure partnership approaches are ethical and inclusive? And what other barriers exist to fostering meaningful partnership praxis going forward? Before I begin, let's consider some of the origins of partnership working in higher education.

A History of Partnership in Higher Education

In recent years, approaches to engaging students as partners, or co-creating learning and teaching, have grown in prominence within higher education internationally, and the literature has been expanding rapidly as both practitioners and theorists seek to understand how the concept of student–staff partnerships can be used and understood effectively (e.g. Cook-Sather, Bovill and Felten 2014; Healey, Flint and Harrington 2014; Mercer-Mapstone et al. 2017; Matthews et al. 2019; Gravett, Kinchin and Winston 2020; Gravett, Yakovchuk and Kinchin 2020; Cook-Sather et al. 2021). In particular, student–staff partnership practices have been cited as having the potential to disrupt entrenched institutional cultures (Matthews, Cook-Sather and Healey 2018), and to foster genuinely transformative learning interactions (Healey, Flint and Harrington 2014). One useful definition of partnership has been offered by Alison Cook-Sather, Cathy Bovill and Peter Felten who define student–staff partnership as

> a collaborative, reciprocal process through which all participants have the opportunity to contribute equally, although not necessarily in the same ways, to curricular or pedagogical conceptualization, decision making, implementation, investigation or analysis. (2014: 6–7)

Here, the adjectives collaborative, reciprocal and equal stand out as cornerstones of what partnership is all about: thinking differently about who contributes and how, who and what matters in teaching and learning. The idea of partnership as a process is also a useful one encouraging us to think about the changes, personal and learning development that participants may experience via their participation.

Of course, working collaboratively alongside our students is not a new idea. Concepts of student–staff partnerships have their origins firmly in a long and highly regarded lineage of critical pedagogy within education. Paulo Freire's (1968) critical work advocates that teaching and learning should be a space in which we can speak back to the processes of domination and oppression that pervade pedagogy. Likewise, bell hooks's (1994) feminist scholarship exploring liberatory pedagogies centres on key ideas of equality and students and teachers working alongside one another. Powerfully, and memorably, hooks argues that 'the classroom remains the most radical space of possibility in the academy' (1994: 12). She explains:

> I entered the classrooms with the conviction that it was crucial for me and every other student to be an active participant, not a passive consumer ... education can only be liberatory when everyone claims knowledge as a field in which we all labour. (1994: 14)

> To begin, the professor must genuinely value everyone's presence. There must be an ongoing recognition that everyone influences the classroom dynamic, that everyone contributes. (1994: 8)

In ideas that can be read as direct echoes of hooks, Freire and other critical educators, today colleagues researching and practising student–staff partnership and co-creation approaches also advocate fostering equality and active learning in the classroom. Cathy Bovill (2020b), for example, writes that 'students' active participation, learner empowerment, shared decision-making, student agency, and negotiation of learning and teaching [all fall] under the umbrella of co-creation' (1024). Similarly, partnership approaches also resonate with feminist theory; underpinning concepts of partnership and co-creation are ideas about power. Rhiannon Cates, Mariah Madigan and Vicki Reitenauer (2018) examine how collaborative partnerships and feminist teaching share values as they serve to reshape paradigms of power. Likewise, Lucy Mercer-Mapstone and Gina Mercer (2018: 142) write that working with students as partners (SaP) and feminism are

> seated in similar and radical processes of challenging, questioning, destabilising, deconstructing, and empowering. We would be remiss if, in our conversation, we didn't tip our hats to those who came before us who theorise, practice, and teach in similarly radical ways – adopting critical and feminist pedagogies where we also find much alignment with SaP ethos and practice.

We can also understand partnership through the lens of relationality; for example, Rachel Guitman, Anita Acai and Lucy Mercer-Mapstone (2020) consider how partnership can enable us to work towards a new type of *relational diversity* in our universities. We can also think relationally about partnership through drawing on how the concept of relationality has been understood within indigenous scholarship. Shawn Wilson (2016) explains that within Indigenous cultures, notions of relations and interconnectedness are fundamental: as 'Indigenous people, we "are" our relationships with other people' (4–5). Likewise, in recent work exploring Indigenous knowledges, practices and responsibilities, Lauren Tynan (2021) explores how

> Relationality is premised on a truth that 'all things exist in relatedness' and whilst this is a naturally occurring principle of many Indigenous worldviews, it is a principle that is sustained and strengthened through practice … it is our responsibilities to kin and Country that define our relational practices of care.
>
> When all things exist in relatedness, it is inconceivable that an entity, idea or person could exist outside of this network, or be considered as 'Other' to this system of relationality. (601–7)

There are clear insights here for student–staff partnership educational praxis. Underpinning conceptions of student–staff partnership are similar ideas that place value on our connectedness to others, and that attribute value to the mutual changes and becomings that can emerge when teacher and students work collaboratively. Once the view is adopted that 'all things exist in relatedness', then our practice evolves and is sustained and strengthened by this value. It can be difficult to then conceptualize students as 'others', or as outside the learning process. Teaching and learning is no longer something that is done *to* students, but instead becomes a collaborative experience. The value is an intrinsic one – a mattering – and not one that can be easily observed, or measured via metrics, or recorded within student satisfaction surveys or research excellence frameworks.

In considering relationality in a wider sense, Tynan also references Daniel Wildcat, who asks:

> Can you imagine a world where nature is understood as full of relatives not resources, where inalienable rights are balanced with inalienable responsibilities and where wealth itself is measured not by resource ownership and control, but by the number of good relationships we maintain in the complex and diverse life-systems of this blue green planet? I can. (515)

What if we extend this idea to higher education? Can you imagine a university where success is measured by collegiality, or the number of good relationships we maintain, as opposed to our publication output, or teaching evaluation scores, or for students, their assessment grades? OK, perhaps this is a little too utopian. But surely there is scope for relationships to matter, or to matter more than they do? Much like the renewed calls for a focus upon an ethic of care in teaching, or upon attending to fostering meaningful relationships (explored in Chapter 1), student partnership praxis is coming to be seen as increasingly necessary and urgent work within contemporary universities. For example, Healey, Flint and Harrington claim that 'engaging students and staff effectively as partners in learning and teaching is arguably one of the most important issues facing higher education in the twenty-first century' (2014: 7). Working with students as partners is being offered as a means for students and staff to reshape the university (Matthews, Cook-Sather and Healey 2018), as a path to move away from an economic-driven neoliberal higher education landscape, and as a counter to the rhetoric of 'student as consumer' (Kandiko Howson and Weller 2016; Gravett, Kinchin and Winstone 2020). Working with students as partners offers a different way of thinking, doing, valuing and being in higher education.

Partnership as Pedagogy and Practice

Working with our students in partnership, then, can be seen to express a relational and affirmative conception of higher education, and can have many generative benefits for those engaged in partnership approaches. The following section draws upon extracts from participants within a scheme of student–staff partnership projects at the University of Surrey. The Student-Staff Research Partnership Project (SSRPP) was an initiative established by the University of Surrey's Department of Higher Education in 2019. It involved twenty student–staff partnership projects taking place across all faculties of the university. Following these research projects, students and staff then published their research in collaboratively written chapters, which were collated and published in the book *Enhancing Student-Centred Teaching* (Gravett, Yakovchuk and Kinchin 2020). By adopting a context-specific, institution-centred approach, the SSRPP evaluated the potential for the University of Surrey to foster a culture of partnership, while also demonstrating the range of shapes that partnership could take. Participants reflected upon their experiences of working together in partnership via a series of reflective vignettes. Below, I explore some of the themes that were surfaced in the vignettes and what they might tell us about how student–staff partnership approaches might work in practice. The following are comments drawn from reflective vignettes on four student–staff research partnership projects (for further examples, see Gravett, Yakovchuk and Kinchin 2020).

> The partnership I had with members of staff was very beneficial as it helped to breakdown the 'barrier' between staff and students. This made me feel more comfortable relating with members of staff on my course as well. They were very attentive to my concerns and took on board my feedback, they gave me the freedom to make my own decisions whilst simultaneously being available when needed. This autonomy resulted in increased self-confidence.
>
> We all feel that the success of the project was made possible through the development of trust between all of us. It was really interesting to observe how all the relationships evolved and it was enjoyable to watch the students grow in confidence. One piece of surprising feedback was how some students were initially reticent about working collaboratively with staff, yet the feedback suggests it was an enjoyable experience. Participants wished that it could be replicated in other areas of university learning.
>
> For us both the true value of partnership working was gained via the process of engagement. Our partnership was characterised by our ways of working. This

was a collaborative process where we both felt able to contribute equally, but in different ways. Our relationship and activity was based upon dialogue, mutual trust and respect. Although great satisfaction was gained from developing mutually constructed knowledge through the completion of our work, the greatest pleasure was in realising that our engagement truly represented partnership working.

Working collaboratively with … members of staff on this project has been great experience for me. From the very beginning I knew exactly what was expected of me for the project which enabled me to utilise my time and skills to our advantage. Throughout my time working on the project, Karen always treated me as her equal, and our meetings were always more of a conversation. When I felt behind where I wanted to be with the project, Karen was supportive and encouraged me to keep going.

These reflective vignettes suggest the powerful benefits of working in partnership. Relationships are based upon dialogue, mutual trust and respect. Partnership is enjoyable and can foster increased self-confidence, breaking down hierarchies. Participants wished that it could be replicated in other areas of university learning. These benefits were echoed further in a follow-up research project which evaluated students and staff experiences of partnership (Ali et al. 2021). During this evaluation study, student and staff participants responded that

> the challenge is to break that hierarchy. At the beginning, you're not sure how to do it, like, can I speak? Am I allowed to talk? Do I need to just follow the rules? Do I need to just be a puppet in a way? Or do I actually go there and say, that's my opinion?
>
> The roles don't have to be completely equal, but you can still be equal in the way that you work together.
>
> In terms of benefits, it's like the hierarchies are broken – you can see people and not levels. (18–23)

Here, the participants comment that working in partnership enables you to see 'people and not levels' and to break down hierarchies. Interestingly, participants conclude that 'the roles don't have to be completely equal, but you can still be equal in the way that you work together'.

Partnership in the Micro and the Macro

Clearly, partnership approaches can have a number of benefits, but what does co-creation or student–staff partnership actually look like in practice?

Partnership practices may include institution-wide schemes in which multiple projects occur between students and staff, like the SSRPP detailed above. They may include ad hoc opportunities for teachers to work in partnership with students, for example, on a research study. Or they may include more structured approaches to whole class co-creation (Bergmark and Westman 2016; Bovill 2020b). Bovill (2020b) argues that such approaches for whole classes or large groups to co-create teaching materials and sessions offer a means to foster more inclusive routes to partnership on which all students can take part as opposed to hand-picked students or students with the time and confidence to volunteer to engage. This is an important point as it addresses the criticism that has been wielded against smaller scale partnership approaches, that by definition if some students are selected then not everybody is able to engage and to access the benefits explored above. Co-creation approaches on a larger scale can work well and can include ideas as simple as inviting students to contribute content to a session pre the event (to share a PowerPoint slide, for example, that can be inserted by the teacher into teaching content), or more developed ideas such as inviting students to co-design assessment approaches, or elements of the curriculum. Examples of whole-class co-creation include teachers who invite their student group to collaborate in decision-making throughout the course (Bovill 2020b). This could be with regard to the direction of the course, course readings or content, or the co-creation of assessment topic or the collaborative agreement of grades awarded. One example of this took place within our recently redesigned Postgraduate Certificate in Learning and Teaching in Higher Education, where a group of student interns worked alongside staff members to co-design a Small Private Online Course (SPOC) that comprises a theme within the programme. Students worked with staff to choose content, to design the themes and approach and to create online materials.

Student–staff partnerships and co-creation can exist in the macro spaces of learning and teaching, then, with whole opportunities fostering openings for student engagement in exciting and inclusive ways. But more democratic and inclusive approaches to teaching and learning are also observable in the micro spaces, and 'things' that make up our institutions. What are the objects, spaces and materialities that play a role in student–staff partnerships? The power of the material in partnership has not often been considered within the partnership literature, and yet, as with elsewhere in learning and teaching, material things always play a role. Through noticing 'things' and their 'thing-power' (Bennett 2009), we are reminded of the importance of an awareness of the non-human within teaching and learning. The following noticings of objects or things exposes the way that partnership is enacted within institutional spaces in new ways.

The first 'thing' is an object noticed by bell hooks (1994): a lunch. She writes:

> If classes became so full that it is impossible to know students' names, to spend quality time with each of them, then the effort to build a learning community fails. Throughout my teaching career, I have found it helpful to meet with each student ... Rather than sitting in my office for hours waiting for individual students to choose to meet or for problems to arise, I have preferred to schedule lunches for students. Sometimes, the whole class might bring lunch and have discussion in a space other than our usual classroom. At Oberlin, for instance, we might go as a class to the African Heritage House and have lunch, both to learn about different places on campus and gather in a setting other than our usual classroom.

Here, hooks describes how she noticed the power inherent in space, and in the sharing of food, to foster new ways of engaging with her students. The situation she depicts is a world away from the standard approach to offering 'office hours' that academics might usually adopt. Here the whole class might bring their lunch to eat together, or the class might relocate to a different space. The role of spaces and lunches in teaching and learning are foregrounded, and become key actors in hooks's collaborative, democratic, approach.

Another noticing is present in this student's description of the process of partnership (Ali et al. 2021: 17) and of the value of access to an online OneDrive space. Student A reported a positive experience of collaboration: 'even emails that didn't involve me even remotely, I was still cc'd into them all, which I liked. And we also had ... between the four of us ... a drive on the OneDrive where we uploaded everything.' Here, this student reports on the significance of the OneDrive online shared space where she was able to access all of the information relevant to the project in the same way that all project members could. For this student, the OneDrive space and the emails she was copied into were representative to her of the inclusivity that underpinned the student–staff partnership, and came to be powerful signifiers of a more democratic way of working. For this student, these small things and spaces mattered.

One last noticing offered here is an example of a recruitment poster advertising the opportunity for students to engage in a student–staff partnership. In the following extract, from an article by Lucy Mercer-Mapstone, Maisha Islam and Tamara Reid (2021), one of the authors (Maisha) describes the recruitment poster, and specifically, its absence from certain spaces across campus:

> While the 'equality of access' model is one which is highly adopted, it ignores the fact that not everyone starts from a level playing field. Communication approaches were cited to be one of the most common ways in which [student–staff partnership] scheme staff invited diverse people to engage. We must be mindful, though, that who designs those strategies and perceptions of what 'inclusive' communication looks will always implicitly bias final approaches. For example, as a Muslim student who commuted to university, I (Maisha) spent a lot of my time in the Prayer Room … it often felt like a forgotten space. There were never any posters advertising schemes across the university raising questions of who was being invited to take part or not. This space could be utilised in more productive ways to benefit a religiously diverse student body.

Here, Maisha describes the impact of the absence of the recruitment poster within the spaces that she accessed, for example, the Muslin prayer room, raising questions of who was being invited to take part or not. Both the absent poster and the forgotten spaces of the university serve to remind us what we might see if we observe the micro within teaching and learning: those things that have agency, that matter, and that surface aspects of how we are engaging (or not engaging) our students. In student engagement and partnership work both the macro and the micro play a powerful role.

Challenges to Partnership in Practice

We have seen that partnership approaches to education offer new ways of thinking about power and hierarchy within the neoliberal university. Education becomes something that is done *with* students as opposed to *to* them. Opportunities for students to work alongside teachers in the co-creation either of the curriculum or in the curriculum itself can offer powerful ways to involve students studying a course as the course develops, and to think about our intra-actions to and with others. When I work with my students to co-design content together, for example, within our Postgraduate Certificate in Learning and Teaching, students are offered the power to make decisions in what the curriculum will look like, and this can be powerful for both teacher and student. Work like this creates new openings for intra-action and can also create new pedagogical spaces in which affirmative ethical work can take place. In reworking teaching and learning relationships, co-creation approaches can open up higher education to more creative modes of learning which shift away from individualization, division and hierarchy. So why is not everyone doing it? How do such approaches sit, or even conflict, with the dominant discourses of the university? (Kinchin and Gravett 2022).

We know that there are many examples of exciting practice, and that working with students as partners is increasingly becoming part of institutional strategies (Matthews et al. 2018; Bovill 2019; Gravett, Kinchin and Winston 2020; Mercer-Mapstone and Bovill 2020). However, we also know that individualistic cultures still pervade higher education, and that investment in teaching is still undervalued. In order to understand the tension between teaching practices 'on the ground' and the more dominant discourses of university life we need to attend to the broader cultures of contemporary institutions. In his discussions on the notion of collegiality in HE, which I suggest has resonance for our conceptions of partnership too, Bruce Macfarlane (2016) describes the significant challenges with how such values are enacted in higher education:

> Ventriloquizing the values of collegiality has become a performative riff in academic life which, in practice, is increasingly characterised by isolation and individualised competition ... Collegiality understood from this perspective is in danger of becoming more of a ... value which academics feel obliged to pay lip service to, whilst in practice they live out a set of harder-edged values more closely associated with competitive individualism. (45-7)

Here, Macfarlane references the competitive individualistic cultures of higher education explored in Chapter 2, claiming that collegiality has become a performative riff in academic life. These words have resonance for partnership and co-creation approaches too. Student partnership approaches interconnect with calls in the field for more collegial approaches to working together, as well as calls to foster kindness within pedagogical practices (Clegg and Rowland 2010). If pedagogies that are underscored by notions of partnership, of collegiality, care or kindness are to be fostered on a broader scale, greater importance needs to be attributed to teaching, collaboration and connections, as well as greater support available to educators to experiment and try new ways of working. Crucially, Macfarlane emphasizes how championing a more collaborative HE is not just fluffy romanticism on the part of educators, but rather has a real monetary value to institutions, one that is often overlooked:

> While collegiality may be viewed as an idealised concept the real costs of failing to provide a collegial environment in practice, indicated, for example, through low retention rates and resulting in costs and inconveniences of recruitment, are more rarely calculated. This means that collegiality is not just a romantic ideal. It is also one that affects organisational efficiency and effectiveness.

Macfarlane's words here resonate with feedback from students engaged in our own SSRPP scheme, where students also described the hidden productivity of partnership: 'partnership makes the university a lot more productive, a lot more fair and just a nicer place to learn and work' (Ali et al. 2021: 18).

Another real challenge is providing teachers with the time and support to engage in new teaching and learning approaches. Teachers will also need to be supported if they are to make themselves vulnerable in relationships with their students (as I explored in Chapter 3). Bovill) explains how the twin challenges of time and commitment pose a significant obstacle to effective student–staff co-creation:

> Time is needed to build trust and respect, and the teacher needs to demonstrate that they value contributions from all students in the group. Whole-class co-creation also relies on teachers being prepared to relinquish some of their power and on their valuing students' contributions'.
>
> Whole-class co-creation in learning and teaching requires the teacher to be responsive to the needs of each new group of students. Whole-class co-creation also requires a teacher to adopt a potentially career-long commitment to engage deeply with each new group of students encountered and to mutually negotiate each new learning encounter. This is a seismic change to the way that much learning and teaching is conducted within universities. (2020b: 1031)

Bovill describes how a seismic change to the way that learning and teaching is conducted within universities may be required if co-creation is to be meaningfully enacted. She continues to explore in detail the changes that may need to occur in teaching practice:

> Whole-class co-creation has the potential to be a more inclusive approach to co-creation and to support the building of positive relationships, which in turn are likely to contribute to wider departmental and institutional priorities of building more effective learning environments, a stronger sense of community and belonging. However, this may require academic staff in most cases to adapt their current teaching practice, and learn to adopt more relational approaches to teaching that are open, collaborative, dialogic, and democratic. … This is likely to require many teachers to learn more about the benefits of whole class co-creation and about different ways to facilitate and evaluate whole-class co-creation. This has significant implications for departments and universities in terms of the academic development support offered to teaching staff. (2020b: 1034)

A further challenge for fostering meaningful connections via partnership praxis is around the concept of inclusion. As we saw in the example from

Maisha (Mercer-Mapstone, Islam and Reid 2021), well-meaning approaches to engaging students in partnership may fall short if they are not including a diversity of participants and are instead just engaging the 'usual suspects' – often those students who have the free time, resources or cultural capital to engage in such initiatives. As Mercer-Mapstone and colleagues suggest, 'we must broaden our conceptions of diversity and begin to see the explicit inclusion of diversity as a mandatory and core consideration rather than an additional option' (Mercer-Mapstone, Islam and Reid 2021: 241). Conversely, we might need to examine whether staff or students from minority backgrounds are being expected to engage in too much student voice or partnership work. Mercer-Mapstone and colleagues' research also highlighted 'the need to be wary of the emotional labour often required within partnership and cautious of the extent to which in schemes this is disproportionately taken on by those from minority backgrounds' (Mercer-Mapstone, Islam and Reid 2021: 241). Sometimes partnership work can be required of those experiencing marginalization, and attempts to include diverse voices can be conducted with a lack of thoughtfulness and understanding of the emotional labour involved. Additionally, in warnings that echo those surrounding the discussions on who is expected to care in higher education (e.g. Clegg and Rowland 2010; Gravett, Taylor and Fairchild 2021), Mercer-Mapstone and colleagues explore how recurrently women may be the ones to engage in partnership work. They warn that 'without careful attention to power, the practices we use to address power imbalances may actually achieve the opposite' (2021: 229).

Concluding Thoughts

In this chapter, I have suggested that thinking of ourselves as working and learning in partnership with our students and with one another can be a useful and generative idea leading us to think and to teach differently. Concepts of partnership, collegiality and co-creation resonate with notions of mattering and relationality that encourage a more response-able approach to thinking about our engagements with one another. Partnership is both an idea and a practice. As Tynan (2021) describes, once you think about teaching and learning in this way it is very difficult to revert to thinking that an idea or person could ever have existed outside of this network, or be considered as 'Other'. Co-creation and partnership involve a change in mindset as well as a change in practice.

Of course, durable challenges to more democratic approaches to teaching and learning remain. I have suggested that sometimes 'hot topics', or movements in education, can be taken on discursively and superficially without attending to these ideas authentically in practice. Macfarlane has described the performative 'ventriloquism' that is used to pay lip service to notions of collegiality, and it is possible to see potential overlaps here if student–staff partnership activities are not enacted meaningfully or in a sustained way. Other practical challenges are time, motivation and support. As I have explored in the earlier chapters of this book, teaching in higher education can be a hard and challenging job, and it is becoming more so as new pressures such as hybrid teaching, and the continued unfolding of the Covid pandemic, make themselves felt.

A further concern is the need to foster equity and inclusivity and to consider anew how this might relate to partnership activities. As the author of a book on institutional partnerships I felt that we did good work and that our achievements were evidenced via the evaluations from participants (Ali et al. 2021). However, I have also been inspired to explore in my own practice more inclusive approaches that invite whole class co-creation, as suggested by colleagues, for example, Bovill (2020a, 2020b) and Bergmark and Westman (2016). Partnership can be thought of – and enacted – as a move against the conditions of the accelerated academy. However, these potentially positive aspects of relational practices should not blind us to the fact that teaching in inclusive, engaging and meaningful ways remains complex and often problematic. Nonetheless, there is a lot to think about and learn from others' practice in this area. Ultimately, more democratic approaches to teaching and learning can offer openings (however small) for hopefulness, as suggested by this participant (Ali et al. 2021: 18): 'Partnership makes the university a lot more productive, a lot more fair and just a nicer place to learn and work.'

Part 2

Relationships with Others

6

Supporting Others in Higher Education

Introduction

This chapter will explore how we support ourselves and others through our relationships with colleagues. Neoliberal ideologies and performative regimes have exerted considerable pressure on academics in recent years, and continue to do so, as I have explored in Chapter 2. For some colleagues, working in higher education may be 'characterised by isolation and individualised competition' (Macfarlane 2016: 45–7). Universities have been described as permeated by a 'strong academic loneliness, and academic life as leaving no time left 'for community spirit or thinking about things together' (Jauhiainen, Jauhiainen and Laiho 2009: 424). Underpinning this book has been the belief that a sense of mattering and connection, can offer moments of resistance that enable us to enjoy our work as teachers in higher education. Teaching in higher education can be both rewarding and enjoyable, and relationships with others are a key part of this. Here, I will consider how we might make time and space to support others, seeking to make the most of affective micro-moments for connection. Such micro-moments have been described as offering opportunities of 'joy in the everyday', and as subtle resistance (Gannon et al. 2019: 49); such moments of connection sit between 'the cracks' of a marketized higher education system (Bottrell and Manathunga 2019). In this chapter, I suggest that there are opportunities for interactions with others that exist in the interstices of our daily work-lives, and I explore how we might access and sustain these through routes such as conversations, networks and collaborations.

Micro-Moments and Relationality

The inspiration for this chapter came one day when I read an article titled '"Working on a rocky shore": Micro-moments of positive affect in academic work' by Susanne Gannon, Carol Taylor, Gill Adams, Helen Donaghue, Stephanie Hannam-Swain, Jean Harris-Evans, Joan Healey and Patricia Moore, published in 2019. I had already encountered Carol Taylor and Susanne Gannon's work and had been enjoying their innovative and feminist approaches to thinking about higher education for some time. However, for me, this is an article like no other and I have returned to it regularly. Firstly, it is an academic article that deviates entirely from a rigid impersonal academic writing style. Instead, its tone is narrative and engaging: 'Stories were shared, told and heard. Vignettes of experience were written, read and rewritten. New stories emerged over night, even in our dreams, and in response to each other's stories' (49).

Secondly, it is an academic article that talks about elusive and intangible ideas like pleasure, frustration and joy. Attention to the affective within education is becoming more common now in the literature (see Beard, Clegg and Smith 2007, or the work from Riddle, Harmes and Danaher 2017, or Sword, Trofimova and Ballard 2018, or Ajjawi, Olson and McNaughton 2021), and the affective has played a key role in the work of thinkers such as Parker Palmer (1998), bell hooks (1994) and Sara Ahmed (2004). However, as explored in Chapter 1, education is still predominantly understood within a cognitive frame, and Cartesian divisions of reason versus emotion stubbornly persist.

Thirdly, Gannon and colleagues' article is uplifting. The authors argue that 'joy is possible in the deliberate way that we have come together' (54), and, citing Loch, Henderson and Honan, advocate for time to 'make space, create, communicate, experiment–become un-ravelled' (Loch, Henderson and Honan 2017: 78). However, notably, there is also a related work titled 'Grim tales: Meetings, matterings and moments of silencing and frustration in everyday academic life' (Taylor et al. 2020) which depicts a less joyful side of the stories that resulted from this study. Lastly, this work articulated situations that resonated vividly with experiences and recollections from my own professional life, in ways in which I had not yet been able to – isn't this what great writing seeks to do?

The authors employ a methodological approach of collective biography. This approach involved a workshop during which participants shared and wrote stories on the topic of academic life (see also Chapter 11). Gannon and colleagues explain that collective biography 'offers a flexible, generative and creative approach to interrogating lived experience and the formation of subjectivities'. The impact of both the method and the findings upon me was powerful, and as a result, I wanted to develop a greater understanding of the role of micro-moments for connections and mattering in our relationships with others.

In the following extract, from Gannon and colleagues' work, the authors explain what they found when they carried out their research study on the topic of academic work in contemporary HE.

> Our stories of academic life, we found, often entailed grim tales ... Teaching, learning and research were almost absent, although ostensibly academic work is about these practices above all ... But we also found amongst and within our stories micro-moments where different atmospheres emerged ... we began to notice that many of our stories were either explicitly about joy being found in mundane environments, or of joy being found, despite the violence of the situation, in gestures, glances, attunements, and momentary flights of imagination or desire. We began to recognise that these were also integral to how we emerge and become as academic subjects–to the 'selves' we considered ourselves to be as academics ... Such micro-moments we suggest, provide insights into how our bodies, and the academic labour they do, are saturated with affects and emotions, how they are entangled with the concrete specificities of material spaces and objects. (2019: 49)

Here, the authors identify the power of micro-moments of positive affect as 'integral to how we emerge and become as academic subjects – to the "selves" we considered ourselves to be'. They suggest that such moments surface how our bodies are 'saturated with affects and emotions, how they are entangled with the concrete specificities of material spaces and objects'. These ideas resonate with writing by Sara Ahmed who has explored the work that emotions do (2004, 2012), as well as how institutional spaces can be physically felt and experienced. How then, in such spaces, might we seek out such enriching connections with others?

Spaces and Places for Learning and Teaching Connections

Dear Karen

Thank you very much for your constructive feedback and for making the atmosphere in today's session so friendly and warm. This has made me feel more comfortable than I would have been.

Dear Karen

I just wanted to say that I enjoyed your paper so much I have added it to my signature below to encourage others to read it.

The extracts from two emails included above are likely to be ones very similar to what we each receive from colleagues and students if we are engaged in learning and teaching in higher education. However, they got me thinking. How powerful is feedback from others when it signifies that we have made a difference to others' enjoyment of their work? How meaningful is feedback from others when it suggests we have contributed to changing an atmosphere, to making others feel welcome or experience a sense of belonging? The comment about feeling more comfortable reminded me of bodies 'saturated with affects and emotions, how they are entangled with the concrete specificities of material spaces and objects' (Gannon et al. 2019). What might be the ripple effects of such entanglements upon that person, and upon others, as that affective impact becomes shared? The above communications are the result of perceived connections forged within the classroom, and via the reading and sharing of a research publication – but what other spaces and places might exist for supportive connections to take place?

Inspired to find out more about how we might foster connections with others in higher education, and what might be the impact of these, I undertook a research study with colleagues from three different higher education institutions and one higher education organization. In this study, we adopted a photovoice method in order to explore the spaces and places for connection and to surface the micro-moments of learning and teaching (Gravett et al. 2022; see also Chapter 11). Our focus was to explore the micro-moments of spaces, places and connections that exist, often unnoticed, in the interstices of the everyday. We particularly wanted to celebrate those spaces and places for interactions which teachers value as promoting learning and teaching conversations, and to consider the impact of such interactions upon teachers' well-being and ability to survive in higher education in troubled times. Our photovoice study recruited teachers and academics via social media (Twitter). Our work took place in the midst of the ongoing disruption of the Covid-19 pandemic. This offered a number of insights. Our participants were academics and teachers, working in a breadth of disciplines and contexts across the world. They told us that, in recent times, opportunities for interaction had often assumed even greater power, significance and poignancy. The micro-moments of connection offered invaluable escapes, opportunities for connecting to colleagues and others. And yet, such moments were also complicated by the restricted ability to connect with colleagues and students, as well as reorientated by the myriad of new ways emerging for interaction within digital spaces. Participants' reflections and photographs provided insights into the affective and emotional nature of academic life; participants often reflected on the joy and pleasure of connections as well as the opportunities for developing trust, creating hope and the power and value of such interactions.

One example of this is a participant who looks back upon pre-Covid connections between colleagues, occurring during meetings over discussions around educational research. This participant describes how these connections take place within a 'bland and plain room'. This academic comments on how what is noticeable about the meeting room is the joy, laughing and energy that was created by the people in the space:

> This room is an example of how a seemingly uninspiring room can generate great ideas due to the dynamism and energy from the people in that room. As a team, we have laughed a lot in that room … Rooms are important, places are important, but ultimately, it is the people in those places who create the energy.

The energy and dynamism described here by this participant resonates with the affective atmospheres described by Gannon and colleagues. The power of individuals to change and create affective atmospheres seems exciting and potentially liberatory. But the atmosphere here can also be understood as an entanglement between the material space of the room and its human inhabitants: their laughter, ideas and connections.

Another interesting vignette was shared by a participant who explored how lockdown created a generative space for her to connect with family members. This participant had an unusual work and family situation in which her daughters both working in education, and living nearby, offered a new source of support:

> My family live in three, interconnected cottages … family dinners frequently include conversations around pedagogy, but the focus and sustained nature of these conversations has been noticeably enhanced by our lockdown situation. The three of us work around one kitchen table.
>
> We crashed each other's meetings from time to time. I now feel that I have a wider network for future teaching and learning conversations.
>
> We talked about the technology we were using, or considering using. This exposure to different online teaching technology is something I would not have had without our kitchen table workspace.
>
> We also give CPD talks on online teaching and learning, so we have been able to listen in to each other when these are running.

For this participant, family members became sources of professional connection as work and home lives entangled. While other participants in our study spoke about how the blurring of work and home could often be constraining and discomforting, in this example, the muddling of work and home was shown to be positive and beneficial in providing new micro-moments for connection.

This is interesting in itself – indicating the complexity of spaces and spatial boundaries being neither inherently negative or positive, but fluid and situated. What shines through from this participant's story is the power of connections, in offering support for both work and personal fulfilment, as well as the affordance of the participant's new kitchen table workspace. Her story describes a unique assemblage of learning around the kitchen workspace with its actors of table, screen, family members, CPD teaching, technologies, food and family dinners.

Another significant example from our data came from a participant who submitted a range of photos of their office space. This participant explained how one specific lobby afforded dialogic interactions between members of the team:

> Sometimes we are in our individual offices and colleagues 'shout' between rooms, so our conversations have to cross this space … at times we congregate in this space to have lengthier and more meaningful discussions. Sometimes there can be an informal chat between a couple of colleagues in this space, so we overhear things and decide to come out of our offices to join in … it is the informality of the space that is what makes this important to me – the fact that this isn't an office or meeting room means that conversations are nearly always unplanned.

Again, this extract depicts a unique assemblage where humans, offices, voices, the lobby space itself, entangle together to create a space for learning and connection. In these examples, both spaces and colleagues offer sources of informal support and enable meaningful connections to occur. Here the space intra-acts with the human actors to create a material mattering. Conversations cross the space and may be overheard or unplanned. In both of the above examples, such connections enable a sense of mattering to be felt; the conversations are 'useful', 'meaningful', 'important to me'.

Supporting Ourselves and Others through Writing

Another source of connection with others in higher education can be found in the area of academic writing and publishing. The second of the two email extracts quoted above relates to a response to an article that I wrote, describing its impact upon the sender and the ripple effect of our interaction (via my writing) as this person very kindly shared the article further. Developing research networks across disciplines and nations has become facilitated in recent years by the arrival of social media. Although arguably not for everyone, I have found social media to be a valuable tool for developing online connections. I have also found that it can be helpful to reach out to a more experienced colleague at a different university, via email, in order to suggest ideas or to acknowledge work that has been influential. Research networks such as ResearchGate (https://www.researchgate.net/) can also offer useful ways to connect with others around writing and publication remotely.

However, meaningful connections can also be developed prior to the publication stage, during the writing process itself. In research on the topic of academic writing (Gravett et al. 2020; Heron, Gravett and Yakovchuk 2021), colleagues and I sought to surface some of the micro-moments for pleasure and joy that can be created through writing collaborations. In this research study, we explored how collaboration through the process of co-authoring can provide unique opportunities for connection. The research involved interviews with academics involved in writing for publication. One of the themes that surfaced in our study was from participants who spoke about the 'synergy' when writers come together to write collaboratively.

> It's usually stimulated by other people. When I do write, it's usually after engagement with somebody in a discipline, and therefore the challenge and the academic writing is usually the crossover between writing as an academic developer, whatever that is, and writing within that discipline. It's that combination which I suppose it best described as the learning and teaching within the discipline, and I rarely have the disciplinary narrative and language; what I have is the learning and teaching language, so that's the sort of hybrid that occurs as a result of that. But that's joint, and that's the bit I enjoy … it's that sort of hybrid, and that's where I find the genuine collegiality and value comes in. (Heron, Gravett and Yakovchuk 2021: 546)

Here, the writing process offers a unique space for the sharing of expertise, and for connection and for learning. This participant identifies that writing affords a source of enjoyment due to the opportunities for genuine collegiality, interdisciplinarity and learning from others. These experiences echo the findings of Mick Healey, Kelly Matthews and Alison Cook-Sather (2020) who explore the benefits of writing as a learning opportunity; Healey, Matthews and Cook-Sather consider how collaboration is intellectual and emotional work, during which writers undergo a learning journey.

Similarly, another participant describes a space in which connections can happen via learning about the craft of writing from others:

> I've got as much to learn from them as they have from me. I think that's kind of what I see. There's no best way of writing things. It's just that we all have our

differences, so I'm just quite interested in finding out a little bit more about what other people do. (Heron, Gravett and Yakovchuk 2021: 547)

Here, the participant explains that focusing on the learning to be gained from reciprocity can help us to think about writing as a process, and acknowledge the value gained from 'doing' writing. Another participant commented on the valuable opportunities created through writing: 'A lot of the opportunities, I've had to meet different people and talk about my research and to travel, I suppose as well, has come from them reading some of my writing' (2021: 544). Writing in our study was also shown to create spaces for thinking, either individually or in groups. Colleagues talked about how the expression of thoughts through writing helped them to articulate their own arguments, and how writing in groups was an opportunity to connect, discuss and learn together.

In a second study, colleagues and I explored the process of peer review when writing for publication (Gravett et al. 2020), and again the idea of collaborative connections between colleagues writing together surfaced within our data. In this research project, a team of colleagues explored through reflections and concept mapping the challenging process of peer review and its often debilitating impact. However, specifically, we found that the process of 'sharing the burden', of addressing and managing critical peer reviewer feedback, through co-authoring was powerful. For one author, 'having a partner with whom to discuss potential actions is invaluable in feeling that resubmission … is achievable' (2020: 656). As a result, writing together with colleagues was again depicted as a generative space for connections and support, and as means to cope with the daily pressures of working within higher education. These findings echo the words of Loch, Henderson and Honan (2017: 65) who explore the joy in 'writingassemblage', and explain how 'our collaborations bring pleasure into our work and engage us with making sustainable, life enhancing spaces instead of deadening ones'.

These ideas also resonate with work by Vivienne Bozalek, Michalinos Zembylas and Tamara Shefer (2019) who explore how we might find new approaches to practice peer reviewing differently, working in more ethical, generous and intra-active ways. Bozalek, Zembylas and Shefer advocate that reviewing be founded upon 'an ethic of care and justice, premised on a relational ontology rather than bounded individualism and competitiveness' and suggest that as a result we may be able to render each other capable during the academic publication process (2019: 349). They consider the value of reviewing as an open dialogic practice, and they advise this as an alternative practice to the usual method of anonymous peer-reviewing of manuscripts which they consider to be rooted in traditions of critique and contestation that reflect colonialist, humanist, and individualistic hegemonies in the academy (349). I find the idea that we might each have power to render each other 'capable' within higher education both uplifting and potentially transformative. Even peer review could be a process that might offer space for making people feel as if they matter, and for providing support and connection, as opposed to delivering anonymous and excoriating critiques. What other connections might we foster through premising our work on a relational ontology, and through finding ways in which to support one another through the publication process?

Of course, these are ideals that we have not yet reached. Moreover, there are a number of reasons why it may be difficult for early career researchers or staff who lack collegial networks to access these affirming micro-moments. It may be that you are working in a role that is not based within a supportive, collegial department and that you do encounter critical and excoriating peer reviewer feedback that has not been written within an ethic of care or offered with thoughtfulness and generosity. However, there are other opportunities in which to access support from other colleagues across the sector and to engage with others' ideas. I have already mentioned the potential affordances of online research networks. Similarly, joining a research society, for example, the Society for Research in Higher Education, or engaging with friendly networks and conferences such as Research Advancing and Inspiring Student Engagement (RAISE) https://www.raise-network.com/ or Assessment in Higher Education https://ahenetwork.org/ are also a good way to expand contacts. I have also found participating in open reading groups, advertised via mailing lists or Twitter, to be a valuable way to meet others and to share ideas. Institutional research groups may also offer spaces for connection. In 2021, I became a co-director of an interdisciplinary research group, Language Learning and Literacies and this has proved an invaluable space for support and conversation, both during and post pandemic. These groups often form communities of practice (Lave and Wenger 1991) that can form meaningful spaces for support.

It may be that connections are available via teaching. Judy Gouwens and Kenneth King (2017) explore how co-teaching can offer spaces for flow and joy to be created and can help to manage the frustrations of academic life, and Alexandra Mihai (2021) also examines the power of co-teaching for developing support and for the sharing of expertise. Likewise, as Bozalek, Zembylas and Shefer identify, we all have the power to offer support to others through care-full ethical and generous reviewing practices, and we should spend more time considering the impact of such practices upon one another. However, it is not just via connections with teachers and researchers in higher education that we can gain support. In the next section, I consider what other actors might play a role in the ways in which we experience academic life.

The Power of Things

> Kick-ass feminist books have a special agency, all of their own. I feel propelled by their kick. (Ahmed 2017: 241)

It is not just people that offer micro-moments for connection and sustenance. In the above quote, from her book *Living a Feminist Life*, Sara Ahmed highlights the agency books that can hold and their power specifically for feminists. Ahmed also writes that

> a feminist life too is surrounding by things. Living a feminist life creates feminist things … We need to have things too; things that gather around, reminders of a feminist life, happy objects even, reminders of connections, shared struggles, shared lives. We might have more or fewer things, but a feminist needs her things. Surround yourself with feminism. In a conversation with Gloria Steinem, bell hooks describes how she surrounded herself with her precious objects, feminist objects, so that they are the first things she sees when she wakes up. Think of that: you create a feminist horizon around you, the warmth of memories; feminism as memory making. Feminism too leaves things behind. Things can also be how you handle what you come up against: you are reminded why you are doing what you are doing. Things are reminders. Our feminist politics makes things as well as breaks things. (Ahmed 2017: 241)

In the above extract, Ahmed articulates powerfully the agency of things as they entangle with human lives. No longer can we pretend that objects exist merely in the background as props to our daily life. Rather, as Bennett (2009) suggests, they matter vibrantly, they have 'thing power'. As Ahmed explains in the above extract, 'things can also be how you handle what you come up against: you are reminded why you are doing what you are doing'. Inspired by Ahmed's ideas, and thinking about the role of non-human others in creating connections in higher education I took the following two photographs (Figures 6.1 and 6.2).

The first image shows the books that sat on my bookshelf in my home working space. You can see from the photograph that they are a selection of the authors that have inspired this book and are an interdisciplinary blend of writers in teaching and learning, philosophy, feminism, critical theory and sociology

Figure 6.1 Books with 'thing-power'.

that have come together to inform my own thinking. As Ahmed suggests, these books have a special agency; they propel me with their 'kick' (Ahmed 2017: 241). Together, these books, and the ideas and writers that they represent, support my thinking and action in higher education and offer a source of support when days go less well than I would like, or when I am unsure of what I am doing, and even why I am attempting to do it. As Ahmed explains, things act as 'reminders' as to what matters; crucially, these non-human things here have the power to offer connection, joy and hope in the way that human connections can do.

The second image represents the books and articles that are presently displayed in a shared space within my university department. The idea to display these things occurred to members of my academic team when we began receiving external visitors to our department more regularly and we thought that it would offer a good showcase of our work, as well as creating a space to discuss the ideas in the selected publications. A by-product of this was that the display area also served as a source of motivation to us, as well as a talking point with colleagues and visitors to openly celebrate one another's work.

However, this showcase took on new meaning for me since March 2020 following the move to remote working as a consequence of the Covid pandemic.

Figure 6.2 A departmental shared space.

Working at home was of course a difficult period for many, and what has also been challenging is the phase we are presently experiencing as colleagues begin to return to work. At this time of writing, I work in my office intermittently and never with my colleagues all together. This display space now represents a past period to me, a time during which we worked together alongside one another in a physical space and where it was easier to foster a supportive and generative working atmosphere founded upon a relational ontology. Our department will soon be relocating to a new building, and colleagues have also moved on to new posts since the last time we worked physically together. As a result, the physical items represent to me the power of connection between human others in a physical space and offer a poignant reminder of the destabilizing impact of our pandemic and post-pandemic working lives. It may be that colleagues are able to come and work together physically once more and that these items will take upon a new meaning, but presently they represent a former time period to me.

In both of these illustrative examples, and in different ways, these things have fostered connections, disconnections and a sense of mattering. These material things could be books or articles, or any 'things' that hold agency within the spaces and places in which we teach, research and learn. Supporting others, then, can take place via human-to-human connections in the physical space, remotely, or equally via human and non-human connections.

Conclusions

Learning from others offers sustenance in a profession that can be difficult and is almost always challenging. I do not suggest that we accept difficult working contexts as inevitable or acceptable, or that we relinquish our efforts to make improvements, and to foster greater equity within higher education; I also acknowledge my own, highly fortunate, position. Nonetheless, appreciating and developing these micro-moments for connection can offer spaces, however small, between the cracks of daily working practices, enabling us to continue and to find ways in which to live 'liveable lives' (Gannon et al. 2019). We have seen that learning from others can happen via informal conversations, research projects, professional networks, writing together, via social media, as well as via our entanglement with the material things that we surround ourselves with. In the words of Gannon and colleagues, I suggest that 'a strategic attention to positive affect by focusing on joy in the everyday moments of academic life' (2019: 48) can serve as a powerful tool to remind us who and what matters in higher education.

7

Learning from Others

Introduction

Of course, it is not just our relationships with students, or even our relationships with colleagues, that impact upon our work in higher education. This chapter will consider what we can learn from others *beyond* higher education, and the ways in which we can develop ourselves and access support. In *Meeting the Universe Halfway*, Karen Barad (2007: 353) writes: 'All real living is meeting. And each meeting matters.' Can each meeting matter? Can each meeting offer us something new to think with? Throughout this book, I have argued that connections in higher education can often significantly matter, providing sustenance during what may be challenging times, and also offering new opportunities to learn from others, or to develop others. So far these 'others' have been our students, colleagues or wider peers in the field of education. In this chapter, I explore how stepping beyond the boundaries of our field or discipline – or doing away with the boundaries altogether – may be able to offer us new perspectives.

This chapter has itself been inspired by a number of 'others'. The first as noted is Karen Barad. Barad's theory of agential realism explores how individuals do not pre-exist but are materialized through intra-actions (2007). These intra-acting phenomena represent a shift from viewing an individual as a bounded body to a body-in-relations whose form is articulated via ongoing intra-actions (Barad 2003). From Barad's perspective in agential realism 'nothing exists in and of itself … everything is always already in relation … matter and discourse are co-constitutive' (Fairchild and Taylor 2019: 1). Barad's work underpins much of this book in different ways, and as a physicist, philosopher and feminist theorist, she is probably an ideal person to open a chapter about working beyond disciplinary boundaries with. In fact, Fairchild and Taylor (2019) write that:

> what makes Barad's work so important is that, although agential realism is theorized from a scientific basis in quantum physics and the behaviour of

sub-atomic particles, it offers a set of methodological and analytical tools, flexible and comprehensive enough to be taken up by a range of disciplines, including social sciences, humanities and arts. (16)

Barad's work helps us to think about learning across disciplines and boundaries in new ways, and how we might begin to do this.

The second source of inspiration for this chapter is drawn from a colleague, Dr Simon Lygo-Baker. Simon is Senior Lecturer in Higher Education at the University of Surrey, and Professor at the University of Wisconsin. Simon is a colleague in my own department, working in higher education; however, he has taught a number of workshops for staff and researchers over the years exploring the topic of 'Learning from others'. In these sessions, Simon shares how his own development as an educator has been inspired by working with a range of different professionals. These include comedians, a screenwriter, a singer and a preacher (amongst others). I wanted to find out more about how this work might interrelate to my interest in connections and mattering. As a result, this chapter includes a dialogue with Simon on the topic of learning from others and what this idea can offer our theory-practice.

The third key influence for this chapter is the professor and surgeon, Roger Kneebone. Kneebone's work has also explored similar ideas about learning from other disciplines and practitioners throughout his career and has shared these in his book *Expert: Understanding the Path to Mastery* (Kneebone 2020). Learning from others, Kneebone suggests, has become even more relevant within our post-Covid teaching and learning landscape. In a recent article with Claudia Schlegel (2021), Kneebone and Schlegel explain how the Covid pandemic has resurfaced the value of learning from beyond professional boundaries:

> The COVID-19 pandemic forced clinicians and researchers to look beyond traditional professional boundaries … The novelty and challenge of such collaborations highlight the pigeon-holed nature of much medical education. As clinician educators we believe that collaboration beyond the world of medicine is essential, not only in times of crisis but also as part of normal training. Yet a widely held assumption that everything a learner needs to know about a field can be gained from those already working within it holds powerful sway.
>
> We challenge that assumption, proposing that clinicians can learn from experts outside medicine whose ways of doing resonate with medical practice but whose expertise often goes unrecognised. Invaluable expertise is all around us, hiding in plain sight. We have a responsibility to our students to ensure they develop the awareness and skills to engage with experts outside medicine, recognising

complementary skills and ways of thinking. The challenge is to bring such expertise into our educational programmes and working lives. (2021: 89–90)

In the above extract, Kneebone and Schlegel raise some interesting ideas about the forgotten or invisible expertise that exists all around us – if only we were to look for it. Kneebone and Schlegel argue that invaluable expertise is often hiding 'in plain sight', and that we have a responsibility to our students to ensure that they develop the awareness and skills to engage with experts beyond their discipline in order to gain new skills and ways of thinking. The challenge is, Kneebone and Schlegel suggest, finding ways to incorporate such expertise into our educational programmes and working lives. Kneebone's book exploring the notion of expertise (2020) also surfaces similar ideas and offers ways in which we might learn from others by observing their practice or through conversations. In the next section, I take up these ideas and discuss some of them further, in order to explore how educators might develop their thinking through connections with those beyond HE.

Learning from Others beyond HE: A Dialogue

In the following dialogue, I spoke to Simon Lygo-Baker about his work in this area. This interview took place on 4 October 2021, via Zoom. Our dialogue has been transcribed below.

> **Karen Gravett:** Okay, so thank you for talking to me about this area of your interests, in terms of working with others beyond higher education, and what we as teachers can learn from working with others. So, first of all, could you tell me a little bit about how your work in this area came about?
>
> **Simon Lygo-Baker:** I think it was probably a combination of two factors. I think I had been reading the literature for a long time and I don't think I was finding anything stimulating or new. And at the same time, I was doing a lot of travelling. And as part of that travelling, I was listening to a variety of different people and podcasts. And it was listening to one podcast in particular that I started to see some parallels between the world that that person inhabited, which was comedy, and the world that I inhabited, which was or is for want of a better word teacher training in higher education. And he was interviewing other comedians about their craft, not about being funny, but about how they develop their sessions.

What processes, they went through, how they worked with audiences and so on, and many of the things that they were talking about in that conversation struck a chord with me, based on the conversations I was having with colleagues across the institution about engaging an audience, and thinking about patterns and rhythms that people used in teaching. And it stimulated my interest. And I managed to speak to the individual concerned and that stimulated further interest in thinking: maybe there's more to learn from people outside of HE, than merely staying within those four walls.

Karen Gravett: Yes, because as you say, there's not been a great deal in the literature in terms of the overlaps between disciplines, and what teachers can actually learn from others doing similar things in different contexts, for example?

Simon Lygo-Baker: I think if you were harsh, I think we're fairly arrogant at times in higher education. Even just the word, you know we're higher, we are in some lofty position, looking down at everybody else, rather than being in the common world as it were, and I think, that almost encourages us subconsciously *not* to look beyond our own boundaries. I mean, I'm sure people would say, well, we do look beyond our boundaries, we're researching constantly beyond our boundaries, but I don't think we do it necessarily from an equal perspective. I think we do it from the frame of 'we'll come in and research and tell you what's going on in your world'. And I just found it interesting to be able to turn that around, and say actually these people can tell me more about my world than I can.

Karen Gravett: And so, would you say that you use some of your interest in the new perspectives that you draw upon, to learn more about what they can show you about your own teaching?

Simon Lygo-Baker: Yeah, you know it was being able to layer into our world different perspectives, different language, different way of seeing things. It seemed interesting, it allowed me to see perspectives I hadn't seen before, or to be able to interrogate my own thinking in ways that I hadn't done previously, and realize that you know actually the arrogance of thinking, well, I can work all this out myself. It was exactly that now I couldn't, and I could have a different way of seeing things through the eyes of other people.

Karen Gravett: So for you it's that difference that makes for a really useful learning space?

Simon Lygo-Baker: yeah I think it's allowing yourself to both be in your own world and outside of it, looking in a new and a different way, and I think so often when I was having those conversations with some fantastic people in higher education, a lot of the time you were just almost talking in a language that you were familiar with, not to say that conversation isn't interesting and useful at times, but there comes a point where you just think that I've heard this before. I've said it before and I can't think of another way of saying it. And therefore being able to listen to a different set of voices and realize that they were in their own parallel type of worlds, coming at this from different angles and seeing differently, it allowed me to find a new set of voices that were interesting to interrogate my own world which otherwise I wouldn't have, because we you know in higher education we use a particular language, we use a particular way of seeing things. We compartmentalize students in a particular way and learning environments, and these people didn't, because their environments are perceived very differently.

Karen Gravett: You mentioned about how some of your work has been with comedians in the past, but can you share some of the particular experiences that you've had when you've learned from others.

Simon Lygo-Baker: Well, so a range of people, and that was part of the enjoyment was to go and see beyond, when I first realized that talking to Stuart Goldsmith and other comedians was an opportunity to open up that world. But realizing, then again, you know, if I just went into that world there would come a point where you'd have the same, and although comedians are all very different I appreciate, you know they still live in a world where they have a shared language and similar expectations, so that you start to hear the same kinds of things. And so it was serendipity of meeting a script writer and then having a similar, but different, conversation with her, realizing again that I could use that experience as an opportunity to explore teaching in different ways. Similarly, with a singing coach, and again doing the same there and then with people who are preachers in the States and again having opportunities to meet with them and talk with them and watch them at work, as it were, and to realize that again the conversations that are stimulated afterwards I found very interesting because, as I've said before, I suppose that you know those opportunities to have conversations across and then into those sort of grey areas with people, who are equally interested in trying to understand your own world, because it helps them understand theirs, you know was interesting, and I think that more equal view that we were both discovering together was also a powerful reason to do it, rather than saying I'm just going to explore their world, and they were also genuinely interested in ours, or mine. It's always as a result of that, I suppose. I listen and watch things differently now, in the hope that I can therefore go and explore another world or another place.

Karen Gravett: It sounds like you've all had all these different people that you've met that have had an impact on the way that you think about your own teaching, are there any specific ways that you can think of somebody impacting upon your practice?

Simon Lygo-Baker: Yeah, I think they've impacted in a number of ways, because they allow me to ask questions of what I do, and why I do it and how I do it in ways that I wouldn't have done before, I do. You know I like to think that I constantly do try and question, what I do, and why I do it, but working with these people, for a variety of reasons, allowed me to ask different questions. And, to think you know why is it, for example, working with somebody in comedy, why is it that I got to a point where I didn't want to keep on preparing my teaching material in great detail? And I'm realizing that we're having conversations with comedians about realizing that for them the craft that they have requires them to practice and be comfortable, but also to live depending on who they are, and how they are, with that uncertainty of certain parts, which is what I like to do, because without some form of uncertainty, you don't know how it's going to go, realizing that audiences whether students, whether it's paying customers, are going to respond in different ways, and then, how do you react to that? And realizing that you know, well you could just carry on, because the next slide is the next slide so that's what I'm going to give you. Or whether the next joke is the next joke so that's part of it, or realizing no that's not going to work so we're going to go somewhere else, so we're going to go to the whiteboard or we're going to do it again, or we're going to deconstruct that part because you need to be able to get this to get the next thing, because otherwise the whole part falls apart.

Karen Gravett: I think there's lots of ideas in there to take forward, and it seems like, for you, learning from others has been a really positive experience. But I was also wondering what you think some of the challenges might be? Are there any challenges that you have experienced in learning from people beyond higher education?

Simon Lygo-Baker: I think one of the challenges is that you have to translate sometimes, and the translation probably doesn't always work, but that's not necessarily a problem. But I think some things don't immediately transfer. You have to have the space and time and willingness to go into places that initially you might think, or might seem, well there's nothing in here. And you also have to have a willingness, I think to expose a little bit of yourself. You know if you're asking other people to explore, you know you have to develop that trust and realize that it's only going to work really well for both parties once you start to trust and understand what that other person is trying to tell you. And it can be quite exposing at times because you know you have to visit places that are sometimes uncomfortable, and that can be I suppose disturbing because, you know the nice little world that I thought I had and this is how it works and it's nicely packaged and I just keep on doing this, there were times when people say 'well you know why do you do that?' And 'surely that's not effective?' So I think you have to be willing to be put off balance a bit, and then some people really enjoy that, but for others, I can see it being an uncomfortable process.

Karen Gravett: Yes, and I'm thinking that in terms of people who might want to find ways to learn from others, what would you tell somebody who said 'Oh that sounds great and I'd like to do that, but I just don't know how to begin, or how to even start to step outside my own discipline?'

Simon Lygo-Baker: I think the easiest way is to begin by looking at the things that you enjoy outside from the norm of your job, that's really how I did it and then you know there's already an interest in whatever it happened to be the art form and say you know what, what can I take from walking around a gallery or listening to a writer, or whatever it happens to be, that you enjoy. And you might ask 'what kinds of things is he or she doing that actually I can question my own practice around and what is the artist in the picture trying to tell us, and how is she or he telling us that?'

For example, if you take the art world and painting, you know you might ask 'does the painting have to mean the same to everyone? Does the artist care too much if you mean something to other people, but it's not what she intended?' Can you take those parallels into teaching and say you know well, 'actually does everybody in the class have to have exactly the same understanding from my teaching?' Maybe sometimes they do, other times, maybe not, maybe that's OK, and maybe then we can talk about difference with the audience, you know we can talk about interpretation, we can talk about meaning. And we can talk about these things in new ways, rather than just within the disciplinary frame. And actually say 'so how did those people do that, you know, what tricks do they use to try and portray a sense of whatever sense they're trying to create, a fear, or hope, or just interest?' And so I would just encourage people to take things in your current world and just really look at them, and say what can that tell me or help me question about what I do, and, obviously, if those things are people, and you have access to those people then it's worth talking to them, and you know that generally I've been lucky that all the people I've asked have been happy to talk back, and that is probably because you have shown an interest in their world, and you know who doesn't like talking to a large extent about their world? Many people will, and I've found that if you're outside their world they're almost more interested in talking to you because they're slightly bemused as to why you're interested in that world you know why, why would a teacher want to come and talk to a singing coach, or a comedian, or some preachers about teaching in their world? And so yeah I go and talk to people and see what you're doing, and if it's things you already enjoy. You know you've got experience of those things already and therefore you're not starting from scratch or you're just looking at them in new in different ways, and then hopefully that's interesting.

Karen Gravett: Thank you.

Discussion

In this chapter, I have considered what might be gained from learning from others beyond the field of education. Using insights from the literature, and from other educators who have played with these ideas, I have explored how we might begin to look beyond our discipline, in order to ask new questions about our practice. After having experienced a number of career changes myself (starting out as an academic librarian, moving to work as a student learning developer and now moving to become an educational researcher and teacher) I have often used ideas from different branches of my own career, exapting them to impact upon my practice in new ways. For example, my traditional training as a librarian taught me the skills to carry out a 'reference interview' where we were encouraged to ask questions in order to be able to listen, not to what the library user was asking us, but to what information it was that they really wanted to know. This is a skill that I regularly use in my current day job as a teacher of university staff. Likewise, my own interests in philosophy and literature have also encouraged me to use texts to ask new questions of my teaching practice, for example, I regularly return to works such as Roland Barthes's (1977) essay 'The death of the author,' where Barthes denies that authors can ever control the meaning of a text, drawing insights in order to ask new questions about the power of teachers to impose meaning upon a classroom setting, or to control students' experiences of a class.

However, it was only through reading Roger Kneebone's work and speaking with Simon Lygo-Baker that I started thinking about the wider breadth of 'others' who might inform my practice going forward, how conversations with others and observation of others' practice might be useful to me, as well as thinking about some of the others' voices I might want to try to include within our taught programmes. This reading and dialogue also enabled me to think about some of the key ideas underpinning the notion of learning from others, and these are explored further below.

Power

In our dialogue, Simon explores the issue of power and equality which underpins his interaction with those others that he wishes to learn from. He explains how, for him, this offers a departure from the ways in which educators might normally interact with the wider world, in terms of the traditional conception of the researcher standing apart from the world and describing it with apparent objectivity. Instead, he describes a more egalitarian process of learning together: 'opportunities to have conversations across and then into those sort of grey areas with people, who are equally interested in trying to understand your own world ... that more equal view that we were both discovering together'. Here, a 'grey area' is described in which both parties come together to share ideas and to learn. These ideas of a shared space to learn together, resonate with other themes explored in this book, for example, student–staff partnership and co-creation (Chapter 5).

Notably, this concept of others used in this context also offers a markedly different definition of 'others' than is commonly understood within postcolonial, sociological or postmodern literatures, where Other is used to identify a distancing, or exclusion, founded upon prejudice. Instead, the others here are simply outsiders to a field or discipline, that have invaluable expertise that may be 'hidden' (Kneebone 2020), but which can be used to learn together in a mutually positive process. However, the value of learning from the knowledge of others that is often overlooked does resonate with the broader goal of this book to learn from a wider breadth of perspectives that have historically been Othered, for example, Indigenous knowledges (see Chapters 1 and 10, and particularly Zoe Todd's (2016) work on this). This notion of learning from others who may have traditionally been excluded from white, male, university spaces also resonates with interesting work by Nomalanga Mkhize, Qawekazi Maqabuka and Babalwa Magoqwana (2021) who explore the affordances of digital technologies to bring into the classroom new voices, as part of a pedagogy of care, or *incoko*. These voices include engaging elders in intergenerational conversation, storytelling and teaching, or non-university scholars such as musicians and activists.

Disciplinary Languages

Simon also describes the regeneration that can happen through encountering the new 'languages' of other disciplines, and conversely, the stultification of having the same kind of conversations within your own field: 'I haven't got a new way of thinking about it.' Talking across disciplines, then, can enable the regeneration of ideas and language. These ideas resonate with the work of Karen Barad. Fairchild and Taylor explain how Barad's work that spans across disciplines enabled the development of new words to think with and new ways of seeing:

> Barad's lexicon – agencies, intra-action, entanglement, the cut, phenomena, apparatus, diffraction – deriving in part from the language of quantum physics, offers social science researchers a new range of conceptual resources for putting agential realism to work to investigate the world in new ways. (2019: 2)

These new conceptual resources also echo the work of Carol Taylor, who encourages educators to pursue 'a patchy, plurality of perspectives' in which 'new-old (theories, narratives, practices) jostle in entangled matterings' (2018: 372). Clearly a fusion of different ideas, and the injection of new ways of thinking when disciplinary perspectives come together, can be generative.

Relationality

The idea of learning from others, in which we might develop a 'patchy plurality of perspectives' also raises some interesting questions about relationality. Simon explained how his work enabled him to engage with a community of others, beyond higher education. Lave and Wenger's work (1991) which introduced the notion of a community of practice has become highly influential in the field of higher education, but evidently staying within the confines of a discrete community can also be limiting. Rather, in this book I have explored the idea of relationality – considering the multiple, overlapping ways in which we can connect to others, be that peers, students, colleagues, practitioners or non-human others. Learning from others beyond our discipline is a further way that we might rethink the boundaries of relations and what relationality might mean.

Teaching as Craft

A further theme that is surfaced in the dialogue, and in the work of Roger Kneebone, is the notion of teaching as a craft. Simon describes how he was able to learn from comedians 'not about being funny but about how they develop their sessions', and 'about their craft'. Likewise, Kneebone's examination of expertise (2020) highlights the fine-grained and meticulous processes of skill development that 'experts' undertake in order to develop their craft in all kinds of different professions, from surgeon to taxidermist. I have premised this book upon the view that teaching should be a thoughtful endeavour, not simply a set of tips and techniques to be trained in – the 'whats and hows' (Palmer 1999: 1–2) of teaching. The realities of working in contemporary higher education may mean that there is pressure for teachers to pursue results-focused teaching, that does not make space to pause, reflect or experiment. Or, as Simon alludes to, does not risk the teacher appearing as inconsistent, or receiving a poor teaching evaluation. But ultimately, effective and rewarding teaching is that which is viewed as a subtle craft that can be thoughtfully developed, and re-developed, over time, involving a consideration of the question 'who is the self that teaches?' (Palmer 1999: 1–2). It may be that learning from others helps us to answer this question, or to ask new ones. If each meeting matters, how do meetings matter, and what might we learn from other matterings that exist outside our normal spaces? These are ideas that will be explored further throughout the book.

8

Becoming, and an Ethic of (Self) Care

Introduction

This chapter will consider the topic of becoming and change as it focuses on the relationships we have with ourselves as ongoing learners and workers in contemporary universities. I explore how ideas of transition and becoming can be used to think about our identities as rhizomatic, fluid and continuously evolving. I also consider how we might continue to develop ourselves in academia, by using texts, literature, and concepts to think with, through opportunities for continued professional development, and by engaging with colleagues within our disciplines and beyond. Drawing upon theoretical concepts from Deleuze and Guattari, and, particularly, the concept of becoming (1987), I explore how concepts for thinking about change can help us, and why this might be helpful for thinking about higher education. I also draw upon ideas from a long tradition of feminist literature on thinking about an ethic of care in education (Gilligan 1982; Noddings 2012; Taylor 2020; Gravett, Taylor and Fairchild 2021) in order to consider what these directions might have to offer our conceptions of mattering, and our thinking about relationships with ourselves and with one another. Through thinking with these ideas, I discuss how we might seek ways to live meaningful lives as academics and teachers in higher education.

Change, Becoming and Care in Higher Education: Some Ideas to Think With

How might we think about ideas of change and becoming and higher education? How might we think about our own development and becoming as teachers and researchers? For Parker Palmer, we need to start with the self:

> Teaching, like any truly human activity, emerges from one's inwardness, for better or worse ... teaching holds a mirror to the soul. If I am willing to look in that mirror and not run from what I see, I have a chance to gain self-knowledge – and knowing myself is as crucial to good teaching as knowing my students and my subject. Of course, this focus on the teacher's inner life is not exactly a conventional approach to problem solving in education! We normally try to resolve educational dilemmas by adopting a new technique or changing the curriculum, not by deepening our own sense of identity and integrity. We focus on the 'whats' and the 'hows' of teaching – 'What subjects shall we teach?' and 'What methods shall we use?' – questions that are obviously worth asking. But rarely, if ever, do we ask the equally important 'who' question: 'Who is the self that teaches? How does the quality of my selfhood form, or deform, the way I relate to my students, my subject, my colleagues, my world? And how can educational institutions help teachers sustain and deepen the selfhood from which good teaching comes?' (1999: 1–2)

This passage offers many ideas for teachers and/or academics to consider. For Palmer, thinking about the fundamental question 'who is the self that teaches?' enables us to think more deeply about how we relate to our students, our subject, our colleagues, as well as the wider world. Teaching is a thoughtful endeavour. And if we are willing to be thoughtful about our developing selves (and 'not run from what we see'), we can develop our integrity and identities as teachers. Of course, Palmer's work is firmly rooted within a humanist perspective. He makes this plain: 'Teaching, like any truly human activity, emerges from one's inwardness.' As I have argued throughout this book, for me, humanism is problematic in its exclusion of so much of what matters within teaching: spaces, objects, materialities. However, despite this key omission, Palmer's work, and particularly its focusing of our gaze away from the instrumental 'whats' and 'hows' of traditional teacher training approaches, is rich in its opportunities for thinking about our identities as ongoing learners. Moreover, his provocation 'and how can educational institutions help teachers sustain and deepen the selfhood from which good teaching comes?' is also valuable. How can we sustain and deepen our identities as teachers and researchers in higher education, and how might institutions support us to do this?

In order to think with these ideas a bit further, I now turn to the idea of becoming and to the work of Gilles Deleuze and Félix Guattari (1987). Becoming as a concept has a rich history within social theory and philosophy (Deleuze and Guattari 1987; Semetsky 2011). It is explained by Deleuze and Guattari in the following ways: 'A line of becoming has neither beginning nor end, departure nor arrival, origin nor destination' (1987: 341–2). Here Deleuze and Guattari introduce becoming as something that is emergent, processual, with neither beginning nor end, indicating the permanence of change. This idea can be helpful for how we understand the transitions of university students into and through higher education (Gravett 2021), leading us away from ideas of linear journeys and fixed timescapes such as the first year or 'induction' period. Likewise, Taylor and Harris-Evans (2018: 1256) also examine transition as becoming and argue that this conception 'shifts the discourse towards an understanding which sees higher education as part of the whole life of the student, which notices and views the granularity of students' lived experience'. However, these ideas can also be useful for how we think about our own transitions and becomings as academics and/or teachers in higher education. If we begin to think about higher education as part of the whole life of a person, and notice the granularity of our lived experiences, how does this help us to think differently about our ongoing development?

By conceptualizing transition and change as processual, and as ongoing becomings, we are offered a departure from the notion of a typical pathway through university, or of any linear journey with a fixed end point. Instead, becomings are emergent, evolving and continuous. We are lifelong learners; a line of becoming has 'neither beginning nor end, departure nor arrival origin nor destination' (Deleuze and Guattari 1987: 341–2). This is not to say that the idea of becoming should suggest a lack or deficit; for example, Eileen Honan asks:

> How is it then that we can create a space to find joy in our academic careers that is not based on the incessant search to fill the gaps, to plug up the holes? Is it possible to be satisfied, sufficient, satiated, to experience joy 'that implies no lack or impossibility'? (2017: 14)

The idea that we might be always evolving, always learning, does not mean that we should not also experience joy within in the moment. Indeed, finding spaces for joy may be a necessary component in our ongoing development. Moreover, as explored in the next section, neither does it mean that our own transitions and development should fit neatly into regular patterns of change, or fixed neoliberal concepts of time.

A rejection of the fast-paced, metric-oriented timescapes of the contemporary neoliberal university has been captured by recent work articulating the value of slow scholarship (e.g. Mountz et al. 2015; Stengers 2018; Taylor 2020). Alison Mountz and colleagues (2015: 1236–7) suggest that a slowing down of time represents an 'ethics of care that challenges the accelerated time and elitism of the neoliberal university', and that this is able to 'contribute some resistance strategies that foreground collaborative, collective, communal ways forward'. Similarly, Carol Taylor (2020) introduces the idea of 'slow singularities'. Slow singularities, she suggests are

> a joyful, subterranean and slow collective feminist practice for working against damaging bureaucratic enactments of power. The power of this agitational feminist line lies in its persistent micro-level work which, one moment at a time, undoes the habitual masculinist workings of the accelerated academy …
>
> Stengers (2018: 81) says that 'slowing down means becoming capable of learning again, becoming acquainted with things again reweaving the bonds of interdependency. It means thinking and imagining, and in the process creating relationships with others that are not those of capture'. Slow learning, Stengers suggests, is learning 'with others, from others, thanks to others what a life worth living demands, and the knowledges that are worth being cultivated'. (Stengers 2018: 82; Taylor 2020: 268–9)

Here, Taylor responds to ideas from the work of Isabelle Stengers, *Another Science Is Possible: A Manifesto for Slow Science* (2018). Taylor explains that slow learning is learning 'with others, from others, and thanks to others'. Slow scholarship is not simply a temporal slowing down of speed, but a way of living life that pays closer attention to what matters, to connections and to meaningful mattering. Slow scholarship is intertwined with notions of becoming. For Taylor (2020: 267) this might be adopting a process of slow scholarship, as a means to make working in higher education more affirmative: 'My own experiments and doings in this respect have been nothing other than forays conducted with hand-on-heart hope that what I-we do together might help make the task of ongoingness.' There are useful ideas here that resonate with the idea of understanding change as becomings, attending to the granularity of lived experiences, as well as how we can develop ourselves by looking both inwardly at the self and thinking more relationally – learning 'with others, from others, and thanks to others'.

Another generative concept for understanding changing identities of staff and students is the idea of rhizomatic researchers, as introduced by Cally Guerin in her 2013 article, 'Rhizomatic Research Cultures, Writing Groups and Academic Researcher Identities'. Here, Guerin draws upon another concept from Deleuze and Guattari – the rhizome. In *A Thousand Plateaus*, Deleuze and Guattari (1987) explore the concept of the rhizome, based on the idea of a botanical rhizome. A botanical rhizome can spread in multiple directions:

> Rhizome has no beginning or end; it is always in the middle, between things, interbeing, intermezzo. The rhizome is the conjunction, 'and … and … and …'

> This conjunction carries enough force to shake and uproot the verb to be where are you going? Where are you coming from? What are you heading for? These are totally useless questions … all imply a false conception of voyage and movement. (Deleuze and Guattari 1987: 26)

Deleuze and Guattari critique false conceptions of linear movements and pathways. These are 'totally useless questions'. A rhizome never reaches its destination but is always 'intermezzo'. Thinking rhizomatically evokes becoming and development as ongoing, based upon multiplicities, singularities and fluid connections; 'the most important characteristic of a rhizome is that it has multiple entryways' (Sermijn, Devlieger and Loots 2008: 637). For Guerin, the idea of the rhizome can be used to describe a new kind of academic/researcher/teacher in higher education. Guerin (2013: 146) explains that rhizomatic researchers are

- always learning
- open to new knowledge
- embrace unknown material
- networked, connected
- collaborative, collegial
- tentative
- modest
- flexible, in between
- heterogeneous
- believe in multiplicity, both/and
- (actively) listening

These ideas offer useful thinking points in considering how we might begin to think about our ongoing development in higher education.

A further idea that can be useful in helping us to think about our ongoing development is the conceptual frame of a feminist ethic of care. An ethic of care has been an important concept within feminist scholarship for many years. Feminist writers, for example, Joan Tronto (1993), Carol Gilligan (1982) and Nel Noddings (1986) elaborated themes of caring and relatedness within American literature and introduced the notion of an ethic of care specifically as an approach to thinking about how humans are all interdependent and interrelated beings. Noddings employs these ideas to advocate openness and receptive listening (2012). In educational terms, Noddings suggests that 'a climate in which caring relations can flourish should be a goal for all teachers and educational policymakers' (2012: 777). Likewise, Mountz and colleagues (2015: 1236) examine the intersection of a feminist ethics of care with the notion of slow scholarship:

> Our politics foreground collective action and the contention that good scholarship requires time to think, write, read, research, analyze, edit, organize, and resist the growing administrative and professional demands that disrupt these crucial processes of intellectual growth and personal freedom.

The ideas rooted in this feminist scholarship emphasize both the importance of interpersonal connections and relationships as well as how ethical practices are interrelated to power. Care is not simple to practice, and neither is it an unquestionably good concept, or a fluffy ideal. As Taylor explains,

> Importantly, feminists acknowledge that putting an ethics of care into practice is not a straightforward matter of treating all people the same but is about attending to women's different circumstances and to how power ebbs, flows and circulates (Taylor 2015). Feminist ethics see care as inhering in mutuality, reciprocity and relationality – modes of relation which assume, imply and require the practical enactment of a sense of obligation and responsibility, even duty. (2020: 260)

Similarly, Michelle Murphy (2015: 719) cautions against 'the conflation of care with affection, happiness, attachment, and positive feeling' and contends that it is time to 'take a more critical stance toward the politics of care', a stance that is not one of rejection but one which pays attention to the politics of care and how 'the exercise of power operates through care in many divergent ways'. Colleagues and I (Gravett, Taylor and Fairchild 2021) also unpack the concept of care and consider how we might practice an ethic of care in a more critical vein, surfacing and problematizing the inequalities of caring practices within a posthuman pedagogy of mattering. If adopted critically and with caution, then the ideas surrounding an ethic of care, and slow scholarship, can help us in our understanding of how to support one another. Moreover, as I explore in the next section, thinking about ethical ideas of care and caring practices can also be put to work in our understanding of how to support ourselves.

An Ethic of (Self) Care

Audre Lorde writes:

> Caring for myself is not self indulgence, it is self-preservation, and that is an act of political warfare. (1988: 131)

In reflecting upon this quote above from Audre Lorde, Sara Ahmed (2017: 239) responds: 'For those who have to insist they matter to matter, self-care is warfare ... You have to affirm that some lives matter when a world is invested in saying they do not.' For Lorde, the practice of self-care is inseparable from the notion of mattering. Caring is self-preservation, and that is an act of political warfare. Likewise, Mountz and colleagues (2015) suggest that slow scholarship can be situated within a feminist praxis that advocates self-care and caring communities as a means of finding ways to exist. Even as a privileged white woman, I can find meaning from Lorde and Ahmed's ideas when I think about my own experiences. If I am not able to sustain my energies, then I cannot sustain my right to matter within higher education. Self-care is not indulgent, but necessary. Thinking with an ethic of care, then, also means thinking about how caring for ourselves becomes an ethical and a political matter.

Practices of self-care can be enacted via a multiple of ways, many of which are explored as recurrent themes within this book. It could be, if we are lucky enough, through finding the support of collective agency and support from others. Or it could be through the things we all know are good practices: prioritizing down time, family, hobbies, good sleep and exercise. It could also be through employing specific strategies. In her book, *Living a Feminist Life*, Sara Ahmed (2017: 244) suggests a number of ideas as part of her 'killjoy survival kit' – including to write permission sick notes allowing yourself to miss an event when overwhelmed: 'Given that we can be sick from the anticipation of being sick, the notes express a political as well as personal truth.' While Mountz and colleagues (2015) advocate adopting an approach of good enough working practices, where reaching for the minimum standards can facilitate a move away from time-swallowing habits of perfectionism. Similarly, they also suggest adopting a practice of 'say no, say yes', where considering what tasks you will be saying 'yes' to can help to achieve saying 'no' to less generative aspects of work when already overloaded. Whatever practices we adopt, it can be difficult to allow yourself to engage in these without guilt. However, through framing caring for ourselves, as an ethic of care, and as mattering, we might be able to think differently about the ways in which we practise care to ourselves and to others.

Peer Observation as an Ethic of Care

One valuable and yet underutilized route for ongoing learning and becoming is the practice of peer observation. If mandatory, peer observation is often perceived, or worse employed, as a managerial tool for surveillance or monitoring of teaching performance. If voluntary, then at best it might be considered a process that is nice to do, if ever there was time for such luxuries! As a result, real tensions exist between peer observation as a summative top-down process used for instrumental measurement, and as a formative opportunity for learning and teaching development (Peel 2005). However, observing the practices of colleagues in a supportive and collegial way can and should be so much more than instrumental. Asking a colleague to undertake a teaching observation, or engaging in observation ourselves, can offer a space for connection and collegiality. For example, Deborah Peel examines how peer observation of her teaching enabled her to progress to become a more critical learner and a more confident teacher, as well as enabling her to develop an ongoing sense of becoming (2005: 490). Moreover, peer observation can be mutually developmental. Marion Engin and Barnaby Priest (2014: 3) explain how observation may be 'non-judgmental, developmental, collegial, and reflective'. Engin (2016: 378) advocates a model in which both parties reflect upon their mutual learning, and where 'the onus is on the observer to learn by using the peer's teaching as a lens through which to reflect on their own practices'. Approached from this perspective, peer observation offers a number of benefits including 'greater collegiality, confidence, learning of teaching techniques, and the development of greater self-reflective skills' (Engin 2016: 378) and fosters collegiality, meaningful conversations and the strengthening of teacher networks (Bell and Thomson 2018). Instead, if used formatively, and if both observer and observed are willing to learn, and to be open and respectful, then observation can be a space for fostering support, connections and mattering between teachers. Observation can also offer scope for partnership work with students. James Pounder, Elizabeth Ho Hung-Iam and Julie May Groves (2016) explore a consultant programme in Hong Kong where students were trained in observation and feedback techniques, enabling them to act as peers in the observation process. The scheme was found to offer benefits to faculty in terms of the enhancement of university teaching, as well as benefits to students in terms of collaboration with academics.

Clearly, observation need not be a performative affair, and making space for this kind of work can be generative. And while some of the critiques we hear in practice, about finding time for meaningful observation work, resonate with criticism of slow scholarship as an entitlement that universities cannot justify, we might also respond, as Mountz and colleagues do, that this 'represents a failure of imagination rather than mere practicality' (2015: 1253). And that, rather, 'we need to find ways to shift the culture … towards a more care-full future of rich and creative research and teaching' (Mountz et al. 2015: 1253). Viewed from this perspective, we can understand that peer observation may also offer a space for practising an ethic of care.

Reflecting on the times in which I have been fortunate enough to experience collegial and supportive peer observations from colleagues during my career, I thought about what makes a productive peer observation different from one that is instrumental and performative. I considered that for observation to be effective, there must be elements that are dialogic, respectful and challenging. My experience resonates with work by David Gosling (2014: 20) who advises that observation should 'promote reciprocal learning; recognise professional autonomy of all parties; be based on conversation; be non-judgemental; focus on changing or developing professional practice; and incorporate enquiry or investigation'. Peer observations, then, can offer spaces for creating meaningful connections and for developing ourselves and for our ongoing becomings as teachers. We might also consider how we can apply Guerin's (2013) principles for the rhizomatic researcher/academic to the practice of supporting others via peer observation. We might suggest that the following ideas be taking into account by both observer and observed:

> always learning
> open to new knowledge
> embrace unknown material
> networked, connected
> collaborative, collegial
> tentative
> modest
> flexible, in between
> heterogeneous
> believe in multiplicity, both/and
> (actively) listening

Observing and being observed with these ideas in mind would clearly offer something new and potentially exciting, perhaps offering a move towards a more 'care-full future of rich and creative research and teaching' (Mountz et al. 2015: 1253).

Concept Mapping for Becoming

Another method for personal and professional development is the research method and practice of concept mapping. Concept mapping (as a tool and as a field of study) gained prominence via the work by Joe Novak (2010), and has more recently been employed by Ian Kinchin (2014, 2015). See also David Hay, Ian Kinchin and Simon Lygo-Baker (2008) and Ian Kinchin and myself (2021). In this work, concept mapping is often used as a practical tool to facilitate dialogue between students and peers, staff and students or staff and colleagues. The aim of concept map–mediated dialogue is to surface beliefs and values. The person leading the dialogue – or the interviewer, when employed as a research method for interviewing – often begins by asking an opening question. The facilitator then writes down concepts onto Post-it notes, employing probing questions as appropriate. Once around 12–15 concept labels have been created, the dialogue moves to explore the relationships between the concepts, and the Post-it notes are positioned on a piece of paper. After the dialogue is finished, the map is drawn electronically and sent to the participant to review. Concept map–mediated dialogue is therefore a collaborative way of exploring thoughts around a specific topic. Concept mapping can be used in multiple ways for professional development (Kinchin and Gravett 2021), and concept map–mediated interviews serve as opportunities for dialogue, where the process of mapping allows thoughts to be surfaced, and connections between interviewer and interviewee to develop. As such, concept mapping can also be a great means of providing collegial professional development. In one research study, colleagues and I employed a concept mapping method as a process to reflect upon our engagement with the difficult process of academic peer review (Gravett et al. 2020). Through the map-mediated dialogues we were able to reflect both individually and as a team upon our development as academics and researchers, and upon the strategies that we had created to manage the writing for publication process. The concept maps served as helpful learning tools to understand our ongoing becomings, and the process was a cathartic, collegial and developmental one.

Additionally, the concept map, as a physical visualization of the key concepts, and as a material representation and mediator of meaningful dialogue, can also serve as a source of thing-power (Bennett 2009). Figure 8.1 is an example of a concept map created through discussion with my PhD supervisor, to help me to consider and structure my route through my PhD in higher education.

Blu-tacked above my writing desk, this material artefact served as more than a simple tool. Rather, it came to represent a great source of sustenance for me through my PhD, as well as offering a further way for me to reflect upon the meaningful dialogue and connections that had taken place between myself and

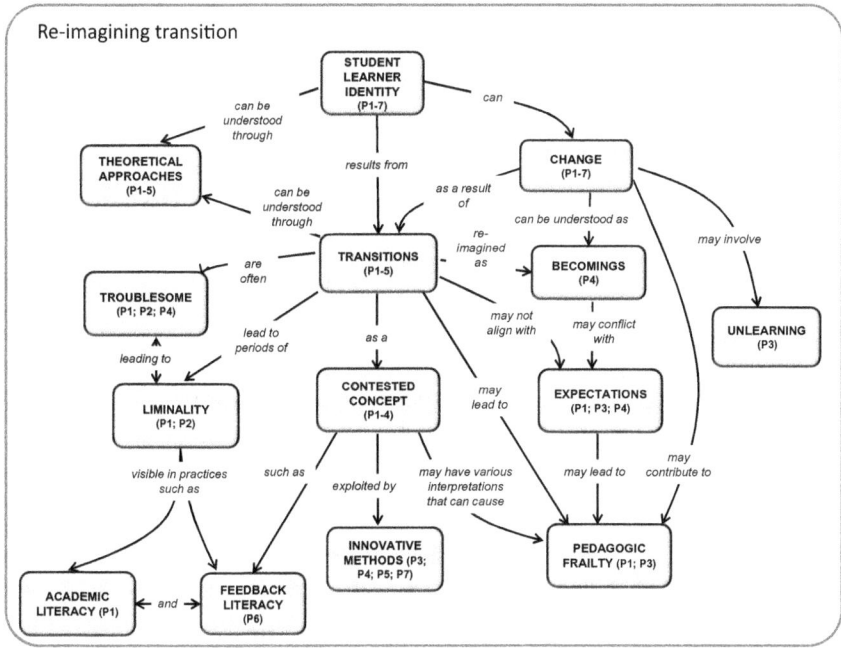

Figure 8.1 Concept map of PhD thesis – Re-imagining students' becomings: New approaches to thinking and doing transition (see also Gravett 2020). Note: The Ps refer to publications as my PhD was conducted as PhD via published works.

my supervisor. Concept mapping, then, can offer a useful means to surface and to unpack ideas, as well as to support ongoing learning, development and reflection.

Writing for Becoming

Another tool that may be used for personal and professional development is writing. In the following extract, David Bright (2017) explores the pleasure of writing and its relationship to the concept of becoming. Bright considers how writing may offer escape from the dominant system of higher education and how 'writing is always a matter of becoming, a matter of the becoming-subject who is becomingwriting, but who is always becoming rather than being' (42). Bright continues to cite Deleuze (1997):

> Writing is a question of becoming, always incomplete, always in the midst of being formed, and goes beyond the matter of any liveable or lived experience. It is a process, that is, a passage of Life that traverses both the liveable and the

lived. Writing is inseparable from becoming: in writing, one becomeswoman, becomes-animal or -vegetable, becomes-molecule, to the point of becoming-imperceptible. (Deleuze 1997: 225)

Writing is processual, and here Deleuze considers how the creative and dynamic aspects of writing may operate as a process of thinking and becoming, even losing a sense of ourselves towards becoming-imperceptible. This has certainly been my experience, and the experience of some of my colleagues. In a study on writing practices in higher education, colleagues and I (Heron, Gravett and Yakovchuk 2021) examined the micro-moments for pleasure and joy that can be created through writing collaborations (explored further in Chapter 6), and how writing offers a space for active 'flourishing'. Writing was seen as a support for thinking. For example, participants spoke about how the act of writing helped them to more fully articulate their embryonic ideas. Instead of viewing writing as an end product, writing and thinking were intertwined, involving a reciprocal and symbiotic relationship. Participants explored how they write for enjoyment, to clarify ideas, as well as for their own personal development (2021: 546). Our research served to highlight and to celebrate the positive experiences that engaging in academic writing can bring for both personal and professional becoming.

Becoming Posthuman

As I argued at the outset of this chapter, my view is that teaching is not just a human activity. Rather, in this book I have explored the many ways in which objects, things and spaces entangle to impact ourselves and our practice, within the complex landscape of higher education. There are many examples of this. In post-Covid times, Zoom backgrounds work to transport us to new landscapes, or to blur the background of our personal lives within a corporate setting. Material artefacts such as books (explored further in Chapter 6), or as considered here, a concept map can work to sustain us, propelling us with their 'kick' (Ahmed 2017: 241). Of course, animals can also help us with our own becomings and development. The role of animals in supporting development has been considered by Carol Taylor, notably in her (2017) chapter, 'For Hermann: How do I love thee? Let me count the ways. Or, What my dog has taught me about a post-personal academic life'. Here, Taylor reflects upon the unacknowledged support we often fail to give those who sustain us:

He's given me all sorts of unbidden help as I wrote articles, chapters, conference abstracts and papers; as I prepared teaching sessions, marked undergraduate assignments and gave feedback on doctoral work; and as I struggled to construct research bids. His consideration, inventiveness and sheer joie de vivre have threaded their way into the complicities, negotiations and contestations that have marked my rhizomic passages in a changing university landscape. (2017: 108)

In Covid and post-Covid times, the sheer number of dog, cat, rabbit, guinea pig and other pet pictures that have abounded within the timelines of academics on Twitter and other social media platforms offer testimonies to the role of the non-human in supporting the work of teachers and academics. We should perhaps not forget that objects and things can help and sustain us in our ongoing becomings in a myriad of different ways.

Some Precarious Conclusions

In this chapter, I have argued that relational work, on oneself as well as with others, can be valuable if we are to enjoy (and survive) teaching in higher education. I have suggested that certain ideas might be helpful to our thinking about our development – the concept of becoming, an idea of slow scholarship, an idea of the rhizomatic researcher and a feminist ethic of care can each offer frames to develop our thinking about our personal and professional mattering in higher education. I have suggested that we might view our development as processual, as becomings that can be sustained and supported through certain practices. This idea of becoming as processual resonates with the words of Elizabeth Adams St Pierre (2015):

> So I don't want my students to be 'trained' in any methodology. One thing that has become very clear to me recently is how hard it is to escape our theoretical/methodological training. If we can't think outside what we studied 20 years ago as doctoral students, how can we keep moving, keep thinking, keep inquiring? I think the mark of excellent scholarship is changing our minds and being willing to do that. I tell my students how precarious our work should be, that we should understand that the next article or book we read might very well upend everything we believe and that that is mark of 'rigorous' scholarship. (16)

According to St Pierre, our work should be 'precarious', and 'the mark of excellent scholarship is changing our minds and being willing to do that'. In this chapter

I have suggested some ideas to think with, but we should be mindful that within our development comes confusion, and that that is a positive, and can even be a mark of 'rigorous' scholarship. Likewise, Fred Dervin (2017) cites Michel Foucault in his observation:

> Like Foucault (2000, p. 131) put it during an interview: When people say, "Well, you thought this a few years ago and now you say something else", my answer is, [Laughter] "Well, do you think I have worked like that all those years to say the same thing and not to be changed? (2017: 251)

Here, Foucault laughs and asks, 'Do you think I have worked all those years to not to be changed?' This chapter has offered some precarious ideas to think with, but I also suggest that in thinking about our ongoing development, we must also be open to being continuously in process, to being upended, challenged and changed.

Part 3
Relationality and the Sociomaterial

9

Things That Matter

Introduction

This book aims to offer an enriched understanding of higher education pedagogies. In the preceding chapters, I have suggested that relational pedagogies and meaningful connections are key to learning and teaching within higher education and that connections can offer cracks that can destabilize dominant discourses of instrumentality and individualism. In the main, these chapters have focused on the potential of human relationships, although in places I have also begun to consider the potential of thinking about our relations with the material world in new ways. In Part 3 of this book, I devote more time to exploring how we might think about mattering and the relational as encompassing not just human relations but objects, spaces and materialities, unpacking specifically what that might mean and what that might look like. Mattering becomes not just how individuals matter, but the material matter of the learning and teaching environment. Crucially, I want to consider what happens when we think about how relations across and between people, things, objects, spaces and texts entangle together and what these assemblages produce and make happen.

In this chapter, I will also consider what sociomaterial and posthuman theory might have to offer specifically, and how we might unsettle the rigid boundaries and patterns of thinking that have long served (and constrained) educational researchers. In doing so, I push relational pedagogies into new conceptual terrain, prompting new questions for educators to consider. Tara Fenwick, Richard Edwards and Peter Sawchuk (2011: 165) identify that sociomaterial approaches offer a potential 'break' or palpable 'turn' in emerging arenas of educational research. However, I am not looking to break, or to turn away, from previous scholarship, much of which I have already argued offers value for educators today. Instead, I think we need to refocus our attention onto the value of human-to-human interactions, and I have articulated the ways in which humans can work to foster relationships in learning and teaching. However, I do think that relationality needs a much broader conception than is usually adopted, and that sociomateriality, posthumanism and other related ideas offer meaningful directions for educational researchers to explore. I therefore support the turn mentioned by Fenwick and colleagues to expand the gaze beyond the social and the discursive that has so far dominated higher education research and practice, and I concur with Carol Taylor, that it is not that posthumanism rejects the role of human, but it questions certain autonomous conceptions of the human and of humanity (Taylor 2019: v).

In the next section, I examine the role of material actors through a consideration of a series of fundamental concepts and discourses relevant to contemporary higher education: student engagement, assessment and feedback, and belonging. Over recent years, it has become clear that these are three of the most pressing areas educators are seeking to address in order to make students' experience in higher education a positive one, and to enable students to fulfil their potential. These three areas will be surfaced through an examination of the micro – key objects that enable us to understand education in new ways – a piece of fabric, some pipe cleaners, a clock, a laptop, a desk. I suggest that these objects provide entry points to new ways of thinking about learning and about the assemblages in which learning takes place. Underpinning this idea will be the belief that the potential actors that impact upon any learning interaction are many, and that interactions do not just evolve around the student or teacher. In her book, *Vibrant Matter: A Political Ecology of Things*, Jane Bennett describes objects as possessing 'thing-power' which she describes as 'the curious ability of inanimate things to animate, to act, to produce effects dramatic and subtle' (2009: 6). Bennett (2009: 1) describes this ability as the 'force of things', or 'the agency of assemblages'. Inspired by Bennett's ideas, this chapter brings in those 'things' from the background to ask the following: What might the force of things look like within different learning interactions in higher education? What effects, both dramatic and subtle, might be produced when students learn and when teachers teach? As Fenwick, Edwards and Sawchuk explore, teaching and learning can be understood as networks of human relationships and material things:

> Notions of learning as socio-cultural participation, embedded in particular joint activity, tools and routines, have become ubiquitous … However, such conceptions still tend to focus on individual learning subjects, and on their particular development through the processes of mediation and participation.

What is placed in the background is how the entities, knowledge, other actors, and relations of mediation and activity – all the forces directly engaged in learning activities – are also being brought forth in practices as learning. As the material is not secondary, but integral to the human, it is through the being-together of things that actions, including those identified as learning, become possible. Learning is an effect of the networks of the material, humans and non-humans, that identify certain practices as learning, which also entails a value judgement about learning something worthwhile. Thus teaching is not simply about the relationships between humans, but is about the networks of humans and things through which teaching and learning are translated and enacted. (Fenwick, Edwards and Sawchuk 2011: 6)

How can we better understand the networks, actors and assemblages that education often overlooks? And how do other actors and relations impact upon our understanding of mattering and relational pedagogies? What do *things* do, and what can they tell us?

Assessment and Feedback

Assessment and feedback are fundamental areas of higher education practice, policy and research and are critical to understanding how students learn and how they experience university. Areas of focus are often placed upon what teachers do (including how assessments are designed), what students do (e.g. how they respond to feedback) or how teachers and students interact together in learning relationships.

A sociomaterial perspective asks new questions. These might include how can we trace the materialities of learning interactions, and what might a focus on materialities offer us? In this section, I draw upon insights from a research study that explored students' experiences of assessment feedback (Balloo et al. forthcoming). In this study, colleagues and I worked in partnership with undergraduate student researchers, in order to explore students' experiences of feedback using a rich picture method (Bell, Berg and Morse 2016). The aim was to encourage students to express their feelings about assessment and feedback practices via the creation of material artefacts: the rich picture method involves participants creating visual and symbolic representations of their lived experiences. This study worked materially on a number of levels. Firstly, it required students to engage with materials, the stationery and paper, in order to think differently about their experiences and to surface their thinking differently. However, crucially, this study also surfaced the material things

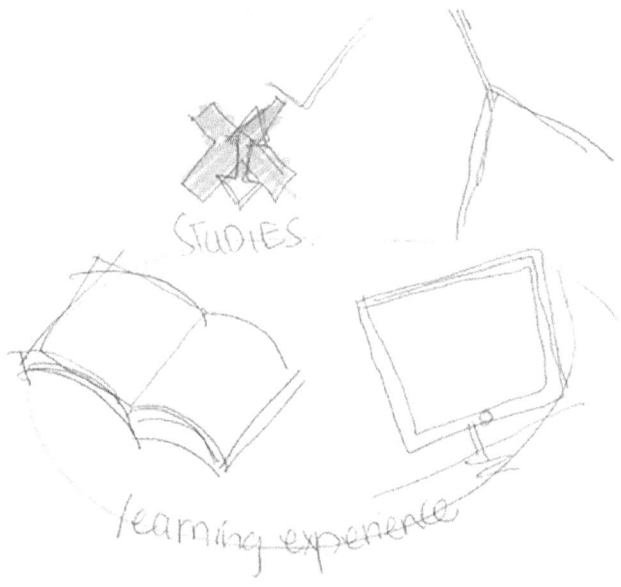

Figure 9.1 Students' reflections upon their learning experience in higher education.

involved in assessment and feedback processes, their 'thing-power', as depicted in Figures 9.1 and 9.2.

In these two images, we see some of these material objects made visible. These included computers, clocks, pieces of paper, texts, bodies and written assessments. These drawings of things operated on two levels: as metaphors to convey experiences, for example, the clocks representing the idea of time pressures. But also, returning to Bennett's idea of 'the force of things' (2009: 1), the role of computers, clocks and bodies are shown to be integral to the assessment and feedback processes. In further images within our study (see Balloo et al. forthcoming), clocks were given faces, or shown as being worn as a necklace around the student's body. This evocative imagery serves to dissolve seemingly fixed binaries between student and object, depicting the lack of separation between human and non-human, the blurring of material and human within the assemblage. The inclusion of these rich variety of images exposes the breadth of actors that impact upon students' learning and how something as simple as a computer, or a feedback sheet, actively shapes the educational process. These things are no longer simply tools that are inert, passive. So what does this tell us?

Figure 9.2 Students' reflections upon their experiences of assessment and feedback processes in higher education.

How does attending to these details impact upon our understanding of the educational interaction? Noticing things, and what students are telling us about them, enables us to look more closely at the assemblages in which learning takes place, to trace how learning is actually happening, and to ask new questions about what might matter. For example, the clock operates as both a literal object and as a metaphor of time. Assessment and feedback, and even students' bodies, become visible as situated within the performative rhythms, rules, regulations and timescapes of contemporary higher education. We might ask what does this tell us about how time is constraining the assessment process in this instance? Likewise, the inclusion of the student's computer and texts as central to the learning experience reminds us of the impact of the material actors themselves within the assessment and feedback process. The computer screen might be how assessment and feedback is communicated, and then it also becomes a means of facilitating dialogue about the impact of assessment and feedback. More than just a tool, however, its inclusion here shows its significance to the students as an actor within the assessment and feedback network. It might prompt us to think further about how feedback is received and shared, about the experiences of students discussing feedback and about digital learning practices. Other non-human actors we might consider to be integral to assessment processes are cover sheets, Virtual Learning Environments, rubrics, digital devices, spaces, texts, textbooks, university materials, stationery – the potential list of things are many. Attending in detail to these things enables us to look again and in more detail at the micro practices of learning and teaching. It enables us to understand learning as a breadth of entanglements of objects, bodies and materialities, and to move away from thinking about agency as simply individual and human.

Student Engagement in Higher Education

What actors are significant within the area of student engagement, a dominant area of theory-practice in today's contemporary higher education landscape? Engagement, and specifically student engagement, is one of the most prominent concepts within higher education pedagogy and the focus of considerable international literature. Indeed, it is 'amongst the most discussed and researched aspects of HE in the last four decades' (Tight 2020: 689). Engagement is commonly defined as comprising 'active and collaborative learning, participation in challenging academic activities, formative communication with academic staff, involvement in enriching educational experiences, and feeling legitimated and supported by university learning communities' (National Survey of Student Engagement 2003).

Ostensibly, the desire for educators to support students' engagement in their learning appears unproblematic, and yet there are some thorny problems connected to the way this concept has been adopted within HE discourses and practice, particularly with respect to the conceptions of students the narratives surrounding student engagement promote. Some of these difficulties have been grappled within the work by Macfarlane and Tomlinson (2017) and by Lesley Gourlay (2015, 2017). In her article exploring 'the tyranny of participation' (2015), Gourlay exposes how ideas surrounding engagement rely 'on typological categories which tend to posit the individual as the primary site of student engagement' (2017: 1). The student is often presented as the primary locus of engagement, within a humanist perspective overlooking any other non-human actors that might play a role. Similarly, the student engagement literature commonly discusses active learning strategies and pedagogies, communication approaches between teachers and students and ways to foster community and dialogue. But what else might be important to consider? A more generative new direction, then, may be for educators to look beyond humanist, individualist and universal conceptions of what engagement looks like.

Through adopting a sociomaterial- or posthuman-inspired perspective, we can move towards an understanding of the messy, fluid, evolving and situated nature of individuals' entanglement with the learning environment. Barad (2007) explains that such a perspective involves an awareness of the entanglement of the individual with their (both human and non-human) surroundings: 'Matter and meaning are not separate elements' (3). Rather, 'individuals emerge through and as part of their entangled intra-relating' (Barad 2007: ix). Barad explains that 'what is needed is an analysis that enables us to theorize the social and the natural together, to read our best understandings of social and natural phenomena through one another' (2007: 25). These ideas echo the experiences of students in the Rich Pictures study described above, who depicted rich assemblages of assessment and feedback practices, replete with a myriad of meaningful, agentic, material actors. Gourlay (2017: 15) puts these ideas clearly into context in relationship to student engagement:

> In order to capture the messy, complex nature of contemporary student engagement in material and digital spaces we may profit not only from a move away from the dominance of constructivist theories of learning, but towards a sociomaterial framing (e.g. Fenwick et al. 2011). This sees engagement as radically distributed across a range of actors, including nonhuman actors more conventionally viewed as 'tools' or elements of 'context'.

Student engagement can be understood as distributed across a breadth of actors; these actors are agentic and no longer understood as simply inert tools, or background contexts.

Space, Objects, Matter

Just as in the discussion above regarding assessment and feedback practices, we can see that actors playing a part within conceptions of student engagement more generally might include a vast array of different objects, including digital devices, computers, internet connections, texts, textbooks, university materials, bodies, desks, pens, notebooks, calendars, clocks, books, phones and so on. Spaces also become significant. Spaces to engage might include student's rooms, student accommodation, academics' offices, libraries, cafes, classrooms and lecture theatres. Or they might include Zoom rooms, Teams classes, Dropbox or SharePoint sites, or spaces within the Learning Management System. Objects and spaces matter, and assume a vitality that goes beyond how we usually think about context as something that works as a simple, passive, backdrop to learning.

Similarly, the teacher and feminist writer, bell hooks, has also explored the role and power of space within pedagogical interactions:

> Throughout my teaching career my classes have been too large to be as effective as they could be. Over time, I've begun to see that departmental pressure on 'popular' professors to accept larger classes was also a way to undermine engaged pedagogy. If classes became so full that it is impossible to know students' names, to spend quality time with each of them, then the effort to build a learning community fails. Throughout my teaching career, I have found it helpful to meet with each student in my classes, if only briefly. Rather than sitting in my office for hours waiting for individual students to choose to meet of for problems to arise I have preferred to schedule lunches with students. Sometimes the whole class might bring lunch and have discussion in a space other than our usual classroom … Many professors remain unwilling to be involved with any pedagogical practices that emphasize mutual participation between teacher and student because more time and effort are required to do this work. Yet some version of engaged pedagogy is really the only type of teaching that truly generates excitement in the classroom, that enables students and professors to feel the joy of learning. (1994: 204)

In this extract, hooks raises a number of interesting ideas. Firstly, she notices the challenges experienced by educators trying to create meaningful connections with their students as class sizes and work pressures increase. Secondly, she explores the powerful impact of spaces upon relational connections: 'Rather than sitting in my office for hours waiting for individual students … I have preferred to schedule lunches with students. Sometimes the whole class might bring lunch and have discussion in a space other than our usual classroom.' Here, the change of space and the removal of hierarchies in offering a lunch meeting has a meaningful impact. Interestingly, the sharing of lunch and the role of food is also powerful here. Such pedagogical practices acknowledge the importance of the material environment as being more than background context to the learning interaction. Spaces enable the teacher to communicate different messages and values. They offer, hooks explains, 'a way to emphasize mutual participation between teacher and student'.

Belonging

In the following section, I consider the role of objects, bodies, materialities and spaces in reference to the notion of belonging. Student belonging has been part of the higher education discourse of policy makers, educators and researchers for many decades. In higher education, belonging has been defined as a human need (Strayhorn 2012), or as an emotional attachment – feeling at 'home', feeling safe and an act of self-identification or the identification by others (Yuval-Davis 2006). Importantly, as explained by Mi Young Ahn and Howard Davis (2020: 622), 'students' sense of belonging is known to be strongly associated with academic achievement and a successful life at university'. As a result, many pedagogical models now include belonging as a fundamental aspect of student success and retention (Tinto 2017; Kahu and Nelson 2018; Groves and O'Shea 2019; Stone and O'Shea 2019). Certainly, for many students, belonging represents feelings of acceptance and inclusion, and is closely 'associated with student wellbeing, academic attainment and retention' (Winstone et al. 2020: 2).

Evidently, enabling students to develop a sense of belonging has become a recurring theme within higher education practice and research. Of course, staff belonging is important too, and both students and staff experiences of belonging and engagement have been upended by the recent Covid-19 pandemic and subsequent move to learning and teaching online or in hybrid spaces. However, is belonging, and its adoption in university discourses, as straightforward as it might appear? What about the experiences of those students who may not wish to, or who cannot belong? In a conceptual study, Rola Ajjawi and I suggest that it is now particularly important to unpack concepts of belonging as a result of the move to remote and hybrid teaching, following the Covid-19 pandemic (Gravett and Ajjawi 2021). We suggested that these rapid changes in teaching and learning enable us to ask new questions, including in what spaces does belonging happen, and where does belonging begin and end? What does belonging look like for staff and what is the impact of the non-human upon how students and staff engage and belong in higher education? The digital times in which we now live, where temporal and spatial boundaries are shifting, offer an opening in which belonging can no longer be taken for granted as uniform and fixed.

In order to think differently about belonging and connections, it may be valuable to look at the spaces, things, objects and contexts in which belonging takes place. In this section, I consider a recent research study that explored teachers' experiences of belonging and connection to spaces and places during the Covid-19 pandemic (Gravett, Baughan, Rao and Kinchin 2022). In this project, the aim was to look closely at teachers' experiences of learning and teaching conversations, encounters and connections. We asked: What role do such micro-moments play in offering space for learning and teaching dialogue and connection, what do they tell us about the working lives of academics, and what support do such encounters offer? In a move to expand our gaze beyond the social and the discursive, we adopted a photovoice method (explored further in Chapter 11), where we used photographs in order to enable us to better understand the sociomaterial assemblages (Gourlay and Oliver 2018) that surround and form the everyday spaces, places and connections of learning and teaching. Our findings were explored against a backdrop of the ongoing disruption of the Covid-19 pandemic, meaning that opportunities for interaction had assumed even greater significance.

Figure 9.3, of a university building lobby, is an example from our data (see also Chapter 6). In this example, our participant described the importance of the space within his experiences of belonging. We have also seen how spaces represent and create connections and feelings of mattering. Here, our participant describes this powerfully with his choice of image. He explains that the lobby

> connects up all of the offices of the colleagues in my team. I have chosen this because some of our most useful and fun discussions take place in and across this space. Sometimes we are in our individual offices and colleagues 'shout' between rooms, so our conversations have to cross this space. Some of these discussions can simply be practical (e.g. who is teaching when, what room, etc.), but at times we congregate in this space to have lengthier and more meaningful discussions. For example, sometimes I have returned from teaching to find a colleague outside an office, so we might have a simple informal debrief about a teaching session … it is the informality of the space that is what makes this important to me – the fact that this isn't an office or meeting room means that conversations are nearly always unplanned. We are all siloed off in our separate offices, so we need to literally enter this space to come together … As a result of the pandemic forcing us to work at home, most of us have been away from this space for some time now. I feel this has emphasised how valuable this space was for my learning.

Here we see that the space, the doors, the offices, the chairs, the cards, the whiteboard, the carpet, all entangle to create the experiences of learning and connection described by the participant above. And yet these material things are often overlooked in our tendency within educational research to focus on ideas and people (Brooks and Waters 2018: 28). I suggest that future research that explores both staff and students' experiences of belonging can be enhanced by paying attention to these material things, and to a wider breadth of actors, if researchers are to understand the micro-moments that constitute belonging and engagement.

Figure 9.3 A university building lobby.

Using Materials to Foster Relational Pedagogies

However, materials can also be actively used to foster understanding of learning and teaching. One powerful example of this is the increasing use of arts-informed practices in education, and the playful learning field of educational research and practice. Many educators today have adopted creative and playful methods to teach and research in innovative new ways. This might include using Lego or other craft-based and arts-informed methods to encourage students to think and learn in new ways. Figure 9.4 shows a picture of a Lego assemblage. This was built by a student in a class delivered by myself and a colleague exploring academics' understanding of plagiarism and academic integrity in higher education. In this example, students were encouraged to use any Lego characters and bricks they wished to depict their understanding of the topic in question – plagiarism in universities. In small groups, students are then asked to describe their model to others. Colleagues and I have found that both the handling and thinking with materials, and the need for participants to explain the materials through dialogue, work again and again to foster a meaningful learning experience.

Figure 9.4 A Lego assemblage depicting academic integrity in higher education.

Likewise, in another activity, a scrapheap challenge led by a colleague and Playful Learning expert Rachel Stead, we were asked to create a representation of our values in higher education using scrap materials collected from around the house. Figure 9.5 shows my attempt to depict the need to support a diversity of learners in higher education, and to foster an inclusive environment, using pipe cleaners.

The process of actively looking for everyday materials to use, taking notice of them, crafting them into a model and then describing them through language alerted me to new and interesting ways of considering the relationship between human and non-human, materials and dialogue. In this particular exercise, even pipe cleaners were able to come to life and play a part in the agentic assemblage.

Figure 9.6 shows a quilt square. This was part of a team exercise carried out by myself and colleagues working within the Surrey Institute of Education, a team of academic developers and educational researchers. The project was inspired by arts-based research undertaken with children, by Anna Hickey-Moody and colleagues (Hickey-Moody et al. 2021) in which fabric and other materials are used to create quilt squares in order to discuss belonging and connection in new ways. In this activity, I asked my colleagues to each consider the question: '*When you think about the idea of your connections to others in higher education – what matters to you?*' They were given the following instructions:

> Please find a small scrap square of material. Please draw, glue, sew or stick scrap materials onto the square to represent your thoughts. This could be anything – buttons, ribbon, sticks, stickers, paint, a drawn on old pillow case. 'Others' could mean anything: students, colleagues, things, objects, spaces. It might be that non belonging is important and you would like to represent that too. Squares can be any size. You don't need to be arty. It doesn't matter what the drawings or quilt squares look like particularly. Bring your square to our research meeting and explain your quilt square to us, like you would a lego model. I will then collect and sew them together for us to make a quilt.

In Figure 9.6 (my own), the buttons in the centre represent my colleagues and collaborators within my institution and beyond. The smaller buttons represent my students. The non-human is represented by my laptop, my phone, by felt patches which represent on campus spaces and by my books. These books are shown as floating in the air to represent the vitality they bring me with their ongoing inspiration. The bottom left-hand corner includes a floral stripe with cats. This area represents my home life which is shown as feeding into the rest of the square via an arrow. Without the grounding space of my home life, my other areas cannot exist healthily. All these things matter to me and represent my belonging and connections to others. I have also included connecting hearts and circles across the square to depict the interlinked connections between all the actors within the square.

Undertaking this exercise was a fun and interesting way to think differently about our connections, and it was great to see how my colleagues engaged

Figure 9.5 A scrapheap model of inclusivity in higher education.

with it. One commented how making the fabric squares, and the subsequent discussion, offered a new way of conceptualizing belonging and thinking about all the different actors that might constitute connections within universities. This activity is ongoing, but I foresee that stitching together the squares will also offer a dynamic way of thinking further about entanglement, connections and belonging.

Figure 9.6 A belonging quilt square.

Conclusions: Tracing Spaces

In this chapter, I have suggested that looking in more detail at what seems initially peripheral – a clock, a phone, a Lego brick – can help us to understand contexts and relationships in new ways. Tara Fenwick, Richard Edwards and Peter Sawchuk (2011) write:

> The task of educational researchers is to trace those spaces, as well as the human and non-human practices and relations through which they are enacted. Sociomaterial approaches provide certain ways in which this can be done, but they are never final or finalized. (183)

For educators, tracing spaces and looking again at how things matter can help us to think about learning differently. I have also considered how using material objects in teaching and learning can help students and staff to develop thinking and understanding, and can enable us to express ourselves in new ways. Working with my colleagues on the belonging quilt was an illuminating example. Although the idea was met initially with scepticism and humour, the practices of engaging with materials assisted us to think about belonging differently, as well as resulting in some generative discussions. Crucially, a wider approach that includes the role and agency of things encourages new questions for educators to consider in their practice and research. These might include the following:

- What are the micro-practices of learning: what are students and teachers actually doing when they are learning and teaching?
- What is omitted or occluded from the assemblage?
- What are the 'black boxes' of the assemblage – what are the areas that we often overlook or take for granted?
- What are the role of objects?
- What happens when new technologies alter a learning network?
- How do things and objects work together within the assemblage?
- How are learning and teaching networks different for different students, and for different teachers?
- How are spaces and times experienced differently, and what is the impact of this for students' learning?

In the following chapters, I will continue to explore some of the implications and insights of asking these kinds of questions. I will also attempt to offer some conclusions and consider some directions for future research.

10

The Wider Webs of Relations

Introduction

In this chapter, I draw together some of the discussions of the many diverse interpretations of relational pedagogies that have been explored and that have woven themselves throughout this text. I consider what insights can be taken forward from this rich perspective and what might happen if we think about ourselves as entangled within a web of relations. What might happen if we begin to look more closely at the messy, situated, contexts of learning and teaching, thinking about what might matter within these contexts, as well as how contexts themselves might shape and matter too? These ideas deviate from human-centred representations of students' and teachers' experiences of education. They also offer a picture of higher education that is very dissimilar from the landscape of big data, the clarity of measurable outcomes, analysable learning behaviours or generalizable best practices that so often dominates how education is described and understood (for further critiques of such dominant discourses, see Kinchin and Gravett 2022). While simplicity and generalizability may be seductive, it can only superficially describe the way teaching and learning happens, moment to moment, for diverse learners, in a higher education landscape that is composed of a wealth of diverse institutions, disciplines and students.

Instead, my belief is that learning and teaching should be a thoughtful endeavour, and one that recognizes the opacity and complexity of what it means to learn, and the fluidity of experience. That in approaching education thoughtfully we remain mindful of the situated contexts of learning, and of the relationships, and relations, that comprise those situations. That we accept openly that our practices are subjective, steeped in context, imperfect, shifting, clumsy and impressionistic, and unashamedly complex. In her book *Personal Life, Young Women and Higher Education: A Relational Approach to Student and Graduate Experiences*, Kirsty Finn writes about the need to make visible

> things that are often missing or assumed in scholarly accounts of young people's transitions to higher education; the emotional and relational connections that take shape in the unfolding of time and in a diverse range of social spaces. From the feelings of longing – to fit in, to connect, to belong – to embarrassment, guilt and intense self-awareness, the transition to university can bring a range of emotions and contradictory feelings of (dis)connection. This realm of experience is often hidden or taken for granted in studies which focus on students' engagement with HE. Often this dimension of transition is regarded as part of students' 'private' social worlds and, for this reason, emotions and relational concerns are seen as somehow outside of everyday life at university. (2015: xi–xii)

As Finn explains, a whole realm of experience – that includes emotions, the affective, everyday experiences of the relational – is often hidden or taken for granted in the scholarship that works to understand learning and teaching in higher education. However, a more nuanced understanding of the micro-experiences of learning and teaching is important if we are to avoid pursuing directions that unhelpfully oversimplify learning and teaching. Moreover, I believe that this is important if we are to be able to work towards a higher education that offers genuinely meaningful learning experiences for a breadth of students, environments in which students' diverse situations are acknowledged and accounted for, as well as environments in which teachers (and other colleagues) can also survive and thrive.

Specifically, as outlined in Chapter 1, I have sought to build upon an increasing interest in the notion of relational pedagogies. Excitingly, relational pedagogies that foreground the importance of relationships within higher education are becoming increasingly prevalent within pedagogy, practice and research, as educators seek to foster a different kind of education and connection with their learners. For example, in her book *Co-Creating Learning and Teaching: Towards Relational Pedagogy in Higher Education*, Cathy Bovill explains:

> Through co-creating learning and teaching – involving shared decision-making, shared responsibility and negotiation of learning and teaching – teachers and students, and students and their peers, form deep, meaningful relationships …
>
> Relational pedagogy and co-creation have the potential to lead to more human and engaged forms of learning and teaching in higher education. These are forms of learning and teaching that challenge accepted power relations between teacher and students, enhance inclusivity, increase the relevance of learning to learners and that enable students to practice and develop democratic skills and capabilities they need in their current and future lives. (Bovill 2020a: viii)

Here, Cathy Bovill explores how relational pedagogy and co-creation have the potential to lead to more engaged learning and teaching practices, that enable accepted power relations between teacher and students to be challenged, and that enhance opportunities for inclusivity.

However, building upon this conception of relational pedagogies, I have sought to go beyond approaches which are premised on the view that relational work exists primarily between people, to take these ideas and expand upon them to include the non-human, and the role of matter in understanding engaged forms of learning and teaching. In this chapter, I draw together the key themes of the book and consider how we can take some of these ideas together and make them usable for our theory-practice, providing new ethical and ontological ideas for educators to explore. I argue that such a perspective offers an enriched understanding of higher education pedagogies that can be potentially transformative in creating the higher education pedagogies and practices we might want to be a part of.

Relations and Relationality

Two of the key intersecting ideas that have underpinned the chapters in this book are ideas of relationality and the relational. A 'relational turn' is not new. On the contrary, it is now a key idea in social theory as evidenced by approaches inspired by a breadth of different, and yet overlapping, ideas such as posthumanism, sociomateriality, spatial theories, actor-network theory and relational sociology. Indeed, Gannon and colleagues (2015) highlight that the concept of relationality has also long underpinned feminist scholarship; for example, the psychoanalysis of Nancy Chodorow (1980, 1995), the moral-development theory of Carol Gilligan (1982, 1987) or the political theory of Seyla Benhabib (1992). Gannon and colleagues (2015) also highlight how feminist geographers like Gillian Rose (1997), Sarah Whatmore (1997, 2002) and Doreen Massey (1994, 1999, 2005) have long theorized space as inherently relational.

Relational ideas are also a fundamental thread within Indigenous knowledges. In Chapter 1, we saw how relationality has been critical to ways of thinking and being within Indigenous cultures (Donald 2009; Watts 2013; Kimmerer 2020). And yet, in her powerful article 'An Indigenous feminist's take on the ontological turn', Zoe Todd describes her dismay at the continued silencing of Indigenous knowledges. Describing a long-awaited trip to listen to one of her academic heroes, Bruno Latour, she explains how her excitement quickly faded:

> I thought with a sinking feeling in my chest, it appeared that another Euro-Western academic narrative, in this case the trendy and dominant Ontological Turn (and/or post-humanism, and/or cosmopolitics – all three of which share tangled roots, and can be mobilised distinctly or collectively, depending on who you ask), and discourses of how to organise ourselves around and communicate with the constituents of complex and contested world(s) (or multiverses, if you're into the whole brevity thing) – was spinning itself on the backs of non-European thinkers. And again, the ones we credited for these incredible insights … were not the people who built and maintain the knowledge systems that European and North American anthropologists and philosophers have been studying for well over a hundred years, and predicating many of their current 'aha' ontological moments (or re-imaginings of the discipline) upon … Once again I felt as though I was just another inconvenient Indigenous body in a room full of people excited to hear a white guy talk around themes shared in Indigenous thought without giving Indigenous people credit or a nod. (2016: 8)

Todd's vignette is an uncomfortable reminder that working against 'trendy and dominant' Euro-centric narratives, which do not appropriately acknowledge the 'tangled roots' of ideas outside of European theory-practice, should be an ongoing concern for all of us if we are not to unwittingly do harm by silencing the voices of others within our own academic work.

Similarly, Fikile Nxumalo's work on early childhood education (2020, 2021) explores the connections between Indigenous and Black feminisms to understanding relationalities that unsettle human centredness:

> This disruption includes turning towards pedagogies that foreground radical relationality and reciprocity with the more-than-human beings, including, water, animals, plants, and land. I draw my understandings of radical relationality and its importance towards generating more liveable worlds, from multiply situated Indigenous knowledges that foreground an intrinsic interconnection between humans and more-than-human relatives, and that recognize the agentic sociality of land, and waters; of all more-than-human life (Cajete, 2017; Mbiti, 1969; Recollet, 2016). (Nxumalo 2020: 39)

Clearly, when thinking about ideas of relationality, there are a wide breadth of literatures that we can learn from and think with.

However, while recognizing how these ideas belong to a wider web of literatures, there is still work to do for all scholars to take concepts of relationality further into higher education theory-practice and to think about what these concepts can do for educators. As Gannon and colleagues (2015) explain, if relationality refers to the ways in which individuals are embedded in social relations, and connections that lead to intersubjectivity and interdependence, then it is a concept that challenges fundamental conceptions about culture and society, specifically Western concepts of masculinist individualism, separation, autonomy and independence. Likewise, both Robin Wall Kimmerer (2020) and Vanessa Watts (2013) describe how the origin stories of Indigenous cultures, premised on a relational understanding of humans' role within the world, jar discordantly with the founding narratives of Western thought. For example, Watts (2013: 25) describes how in the story of Genesis, the interaction of Eve and the Serpent, results in shame and excommunication from nature meaning that future dialogue and communication with animals becomes taboo: 'It is at this point of conflict where thought, perception, and action are separated from the supposed inertia of nature.' While, conversely, in many Indigenous origin stories,

> the idea that humans were the last species to arrive on earth was central; it also meant that humans arrived in a state of dependence on an already-functioning society. The inclusion of humans into this society meant that certain agreements, arrangements, etc. had to be made with the animal world, plant world, sky world, mineral world and other non-human species. (Watts 2013: 25)

These fundamental stories shape our thinking and the ways in which we view our relations and responsibilities to one another and to animal and material others. Crucially, they can also be used to think entirely differently about relational pedagogies and about mattering and connections within higher education.

Another key theoretical idea that can be used to understand these ideas further is Karen Barad's concept of intra-action (2007) (see also Chapter 1). Barad creates the neologism of 'intra-action', as opposed to interaction, to suggest that the 'self' comes into being in relation with and through the entanglement of, oneself with others, whether human, non-human or environmental. For Barad, individuals do not pre-exist the event but are materialized through intra-actions that constitute the event. She argues, 'It is through specific agential intra-actions that the boundaries and properties of the "components" of phenomena become determinate and that particular embodied concepts become meaningful' (Barad 2003: 815). Intra-action represents an ontological shift from viewing an individual as a bounded body to a body in relations whose form is articulated via ongoing intra-actions (Barad 2003). Events, or phenomena, are produced by material-discursive intra-actions which acknowledge both discourse and matter. From Barad's perspective 'nothing exists in and of itself … everything is always already in relation ... matter and discourse are co-constitutive' (Fairchild and Taylor 2019: 1).

Similarly, another generative idea is the notion of affirmative ethics (Braidotti 2013). Affirmative ethics provides a means to consider what is produced by relational pedagogies and how this plays out within staff and student relationships. Affirmative ethics 'is based on the praxis of constructing positivity, thus propelling new social conditions and relations into being' (Braidotti 2013: 129). Considering the affirmative within higher education is, wherever possible, about orienting to modes of knowledge production and ways of acting that are collaborative and non-competitive. Donna Haraway's (1988, 1997) work, and her notion of response-ability, has also been influential in shaping a more situated relational perspective on knowledge. Haraway describes response-ability as a relational process. Rather than responsibility which evokes paternalistic ideas of being responsible for another, and intimates a dimension of power-over, response-ability focuses on our ability to respond, to act and how we might learn to be more responsive to others. An ontology of response-ability involves an acknowledgement of situated practices. In posthuman thinking, response-ability and pedagogy are intertwined as they 'constitute relational processes through which social, political, and material entanglements in higher education ... are rendered capable through each other to bring about social transformation' (Bozalek and Zembylas 2017: 64). Practically, we might see these concepts of response-ability, intra-action or affirmative ethics as offering new directions for how we understand engagement with students.

These ideas, which break down 'the corporeal and theoretical borders of the epistemological-ontological divide' (Watts 2013: 26) also resonate with work examining the (overlooked) role of bodies, affect and emotions in education. As we shift further away from dominant discourses that uphold a Cartesian separation of reason and emotion in separate spheres, the role that emotions play in learning is being understood to be critically important within education. Understanding how emotions work in learning and teaching, and what role they might play within connections and relational pedagogies matters. But what roles emotions play, and what emotions even are, is still extremely nebulous and much debated. In her book, *The Cultural Politics of Emotions*, Sara Ahmed (2004) offers new and radical insights for our understanding of emotions as cultural and social as opposed to internal, even critiquing the binaries between inside and outside. Ahmed asks us to look at how emotions are felt collectively, their impact physically and upon bodies, as well as to ask what do emotions do? Emotions and the work that they do in higher education play a key role in research by Beard, Clegg and Smith (2007), Taylor and colleagues (2020) and Gannon and colleagues (2019). It also informs work on feedback in higher education (Shields 2015), and work examining higher education by Sue Clegg (2013), who suggests that universities themselves can be understood as marked by the 'discursive erasure of emotion', while at the same time deploying affective economies that reinforce privilege and disproportionately disadvantage women (75–6). Emotions pervade and flow within organizations in complex ways; emotions matter. Crucially, authors agree that practices like kindness and friendship can work against the oppressive constraints of neoliberal universities and can subvert neoliberal practices and logic (Clegg 2009; Clegg and Rowland 2010). Relationships matter.

What Are the Implications for Pedagogy and Practice?

Evidently, the implications of thinking about relationality, and of moving away from individualistic narratives funded upon cognitivism and humanism, are many. Palmer writes that a good teacher must weave 'a web of connectedness' (1998: 67). But what does this web look like and how do we weave it? This book has explored the multiple ways in which concepts of relationality and connectedness might be put to work in practice. This might involve exploring vulnerability as relational pedagogy, connecting with students through developing trust and authenticity, working together with students through co-creation and student–staff partnership approaches, as well as through connecting to others in order to support and develop our own selves as teachers. Within this connected web, I have explored the role of things, objects and materialities: how things matter, and how things and people come together within the complex assemblages of learning and teaching.

And yet, key challenges remain to thinking and doing learning and teaching in this way. Higher education is still founded upon notions of individuality. In this article by Fawns and colleagues (Fawns et al. 2022), we discuss the problem of the 'superstar' teacher: the challenge of the increasing prominence of teaching awards rewarding a few high-profile individuals in the sector, and the impact of this upon those many excellent teachers who are not rewarded. This can be seen as an example of the entanglement of the human with the material, where a physical award shapes the ways in which we think and talk about both individual teachers, as well as materializing the profession of teaching in new ways. Not only do individualistic approaches silence the success of others but they also work to construct the meaning of what teaching is to be something individual; enacted alone; discernible through measurable, visible, tangible, outcomes; and discursively represented by individual teachers. This resonates with ideas explored in Chapter 2, which considers the wider context in which this book is situated, including the constraints of neoliberalism, marketization, and how ideas of connectedness and collegiality may appear antithetical to the real day-to-day environments in which we work.

In an article that enabled some of the embryonic ideas of this book, on the pedagogies of mattering in higher education, myself and colleagues take these ideas further and sketch out how we might make them usable as educators in our daily theory-practice by exploring the concept of pedagogies of mattering (Gravett, Taylor and Fairchild 2021). Pedagogies of mattering expand the scope of what matters to include a multiplicity of actors, drawing attention to how these actors are situated together in relational practices, and it urges detailed attention to micro-level events. Pedagogies of mattering conceptually broadens the current framing of relational pedagogies in some important ways, offering new insights into how learning is experienced, how staff and students' relations are entangled with care and how the affective informs the everyday life of higher education institutions. Pedagogies of mattering illuminate how teaching and learning relations are entangled with matters of power, and how inequalities are produced through the relations of bodies, spaces and materialities. For example, in the following extract we consider what the impact of attending to 'thing power' might be for learning and teaching:

> When campuses were offering face-to-face teaching, masks were de rigeur, many of us also wore gloves when doing in-person teaching. How do these things influence pedagogy? How do they shape conditions in which care matters? The move to online teaching saw the relationality between bodies become mediated by laptops, tablets and smartphones. In these liminal online spaces, anonymous bodies appear, ephemeral and ghostly, as cameras are turned off – a gallery of black squares populated by a student name, an email or a phone number. These online relational bodies lack physical form; all online participants (staff and students) are bodies without physical boundaries (Haraway 2004) … Enacting pedagogies of mattering can tune us into how normative learning and teaching relations are shaped by object-space arrangements in classrooms which impact student-staff relations and produce visible and unknown and hidden in/ex/clusions. (Gravett, Taylor and Fairchild 2021: 9–10)

Similarly, attending to relationality and mattering can impact upon the ways in which we think about assessment:

> The first is to try to diminish the notion that assessment is something that is 'done to' students. Posthumanism encourages us to position assessment as, instead, a material-discursive doing. This entails designing assessments in which students have a stake, in which what is assessed does not appear as if it were a disembodied thing that exists 'outside' or 'beyond' them but as a process in which they can participate in meaningful ways. (2021: 12)

Pedagogies of mattering may help us to foster more caring and ethical ways of working with students by encouraging us to notice our institutions and learning spaces anew: as assemblages where heterogeneous bodies – human and non-human, social, material – connect and interact and in which, through their continual flux, positive change (if not transformation) can take hold.

Conclusions

Changing the ways in which we teach, and the ways we think about teaching, requires a significant cultural and ideological shift. This leads us to ask new questions about what we mean by key concepts such as student engagement, relationships and connections; it leads to new practices and to alternative ways of thinking about power, and it destabilizes our conceptions of the notion of individuals and collectives. Thinking and doing education differently, or education as the practice of freedom (hooks 1994), is always going to be accompanied by challenges. This book has developed some new ideas in terms of the ways in which we might think about ourselves as teachers, and such ideas are inevitably not going to be received well by all! I clearly remember the surprise of one member of staff, who in a class where we explored how we might co-create curricula with students responded, 'But why would I want to do that?' A valid question. This episode then also reminded me of an earlier incident in my career, when I worked as an academic librarian attached to a faculty. Keen to contribute to the effective running of the academic programmes in which I supported, I accepted an invitation to attend a Course Board of Studies meeting, only to be greeted rudely by one disciplinary academic colleague who looked at me and exclaimed, 'Why is the Librarian here!?' For many, educational hierarchies, and whose voices are included in the decisions surrounding teaching, are not up for debate, and new ways of thinking about who and what matters may be experienced as deeply affronting to their own values. This is not to say that their values are wrong. But while I would not suggest this, I would instead ask what value is there in excluding the voices of others, or in keeping the control of learning and teaching in the hands of the few, the already powerful? Whose voices does this silence, and how does this silencing serve our diverse student body?

Of course, conventional notions about who and what matters still hold strong. The term 'student-centred' or 'learner-centred' predominates, as does the concept of a singular student experience. Although I have also used terms such as student-centred myself in the past, I now feel that such concepts are not helpful if you adopt a view in which relations, and connections and collectives, matter, and which problematizes discourses in which any one person or thing is granted centre stage. Rather, pedagogies of mattering require a movement away from binaries. A more nuanced conception of relational pedagogies also problematizes simple notions of care, emotions or ideas of belonging and inclusivity as being straightforward. We cannot assume emotions are neutral, or care is simple or always positive. We can't ignore the role of the material or the non-human. Where else might we be able to see it? Such ideas also bring with it a new excitement. Spaces to get excited about the role of theory in teaching and learning. Spaces to get excited about the role of educational research. New directions of thinking about the impact of the micro, and a movement away from metrics and towards mattering.

This book has brought together a number of ideas, theories and practical examples to think about connections, mattering and relational pedagogies in new ways. My hope is that these new ways will offer inspiration or support to educators who want to change their practice, or who are already thinking similarly, but might feel alone in their wish to enact learning and teaching differently in higher education. My aim is also to open up a dialogue and to engage in wider conversations surrounding the role of relations, connections and mattering in higher education. This book seeks to contribute to a wider web of other valuable and generative work. It looks to build upon the 'tangled roots' (Todd 2016) of a diversity of scholars, whose voices are upending the boundaries of what matters in learning and teaching, as well as critiquing notions of individuality and the relational and how we might use these ideas to think about who and what matters. While I have provided case studies, ideas and examples, there is a need for further research and practice to continue to bend the boundaries of what is possible for imagining how teaching and learning in higher education might be. In the final chapter, I explore some of the challenges ahead, and I consider how we might respond to critiques from those teachers and colleagues who think that relational pedagogies are not worthwhile or cannot be done. I then move on to consider some of the new directions for research in this area, and the next steps for thinking about connections and mattering in higher education.

11

Conclusions and Directions for Future Research

Introduction

This book closes by considering future agendas for theory-practice within the field of higher education and with a particular focus on relational pedagogies. This might include experimenting with new and innovative research methods, it might involve engaging some of the theories considered in this book in original ways, or it might involve other approaches to adopting relational pedagogies. How might we take forward some of the ideas explored in this book, and what might this achieve? What are the insights and implications for understanding mattering in higher education?

Insights for Theory-Practice

One of the key directions for advancing the ideas discussed in this book, and developing them in new directions, is via further research. There are a number of innovative and emerging research methods that work effectively with some of the theories and perspectives I have examined, as ways to think about relationships, connections and mattering. Rachael Dwyer and Alison Black (2021) discuss how contemplative, arts-based and storied methodologies, in particular, enable us to understand and see different points of view, as well as to dismantle the idea that personal and professional lives are not intricately entangled. In this section, I explore a breadth of contemplative, arts-based, visual, ethnographic and storied methodologies in order to consider further how they may be useful to our thinking.

One interesting example is work that has begun to adopt fine-grained ethnographic approaches to understand students' everyday experiences. Research by Lesley Gourlay and Martin Oliver (2016, 2018) engages sociomaterial theory together with ethnographic methods, for example, using a multimodal journaling approach. One specific example of this method involved student participants being given iPod Touch devices and asked to document their day-to-day practices and interactions with texts and technologies (Gourlay and Oliver 2016). Participants were asked to attend interviews in order to discuss these practices. As part of this, students were also asked to create drawings of the places and resources where they had studied, and these drawings formed the basis for discussion. Gourlay and Oliver describe how students were invited to create journals of their practice, constituted through a variety of multimodal data. They explain how this method enabled the students to create and share the assemblages that constituted their learning: 'In addition, many participants brought in the material artefacts of their practices, presenting these alongside the digitised words and images that they had curated. These included books, notebooks, highlighter pens, post-it notes, folders, printed papers and completed surveys' (Gourlay and Oliver 2016: 304). This study, and the visual, sociomaterial, inspired approach adopted, enabled the researchers to surface some of the less visible, everyday, practices that underpin student engagement in new ways. It enabled them to examine what actors are involved in students' relationships with the digital, and what connections exist between humans, computers, spaces and objects as students learn.

In their study, Gourlay and Oliver (2016) explore how visual methodologies are especially useful in understanding the complexity of learning practices, as they can allow for the deployment of images in a way that offers several advantages, and how they can also work well within a sociomaterial approach. This was a direction that myself and colleagues also wanted to pursue, and we did so by experimenting with another visual method: photovoice (Wass et al. 2020; Gravett et al. 2022). Photovoice methods involve paying attention, not to just the words of what human participants say (as in interviews or focus groups) but to the wider contexts in which research happens. This inevitably includes spaces, things and objects, and prompts a focus on the relationality and connections that underpin the research process. The photovoice method is also a participatory approach that holds value for eliciting different stories from that which can be gleaned by more commonly adopted research methods such as interviews (Wass et al. 2020). One of the key aims of photovoice research is to disrupt power binaries between researcher/participant and to engage participants actively within the research, via the submission of their own photographs as data (or 'voices'). As such, it is a method which 'asks participants to take photographs of things they associate with and/or practice as part of the community to which they belong, and thus give "voice" to their collective experiences for the purposes of knowledge creation' (Waight 2020: 180). As a participatory research approach, photovoice also offers the scope to enable the surfacing of voices from discrete and under-represented communities (Liebenburg 2018). In a recent work using photovoice (Gravett et al. 2022), we considered the places, spaces and entanglements of pedagogical conversations in new ways, and including photographs as a key part of our dataset enabled us to surface the sociomaterial contexts of learning and connections. Participants were asked to submit photographs that they think captured a learning and teaching conversation that had been meaningful to them. Participants were asked to submit their photograph along with a reflective piece detailing why they had chosen the particular image and how this was valuable to them. The images then became a reference point for participants to reflect upon the spaces, objects and people they identified as being important within their learning and teaching encounters.

Another generative, visual method for thinking about connections and mattering in higher education differently is video blogging. Video blogging, or vlogging, also offers an innovative opportunity to engage digital media, moving beyond the focus on language within educational research, and widening the gaze to the broader actors involved in learning. In work I am undertaking with two colleagues, Rola Ajjawi and Sarah O'Shea, and inspired by the recent work of Sarah O'Shea (2020, 2021) using visual research methods, we invited student participants to create a series of vlogs that depict the day-to-day lived experiences of being an undergraduate student. Vlogs are an effective way of exploring lived experiences within a specific context or situation. These short video narratives can be recorded simply by the student themselves, with the video function on a mobile phone, and can then be accompanied by a short self-narration on the identified theme. To assist students in the narration, we provided participants with a series of questions or conversation starters that 'frame' the focus of the vlog. The conversation starters included the following:

- Tell us what a 'typical' day of study might look like for you.
- Tell or show us your learning spaces? What specific objects (table, bed, screen, laptop, mug, pet, etc.) do you need when studying.
- What does belonging look and feel like in these spaces.
- Who/what helps you to belong to the course, university.

The use of digital media and the combination of both audio and visual will, we hope, provide a more holistic overview of students' experiences. Further examples of vlogs are available here: https://www.ncsehe.edu.au/my-story-student-voice-reflections-2020-ncsehe-vloggers/.

Likewise, arts-informed approaches can also enable the development of generative research methods that resonate with sociomaterial or posthuman sensibilities. In Chapter 9, I explored the arts-informed method of patchwork quilting, inspired by work by Anna Hickey-Moody and colleagues (2021) to conceptualize teacher belonging in higher education. A further visual and arts-informed method to understand teachers' experiences is data visualization. Experimenting with new ways to think about mattering, and about datafication in education, Cathy Burnett, Guy Merchant and Ian Guest's work (2021) offers an innovative way to collect 'small' quantitative data, and to use this to surface mattering and connections in education. Responding to sectoral preoccupations with big data, metricization and how this landscape has impacted teachers, Burnett, Merchant and Guest (2021: 1) explore how generating 'small' data, visualized on postcards, might 'recalibrate teachers' relations with data, foregrounding relational, embodied and ethical dimensions of teaching'. In this research, Burnett, Merchant and Guest invited primary school teachers to participate in an introductory workshop to explore approaches to visualizing data, looking at examples of creative visualizations (David McCandless 2010) and then experimenting with quantifying experiences. Over the course of an academic year, participants were invited to create six postcards, collecting data on aspects of their experience that mattered to them, for example, how many scripts marked, and then visualizing these data through illustrations on their postcards. At regular meetings, teachers discussed what their postcards represented. Using this innovative method, Bennett, Merchant and Guest were able to surface notions of teacher mattering in imaginative ways. This method offers new insights into educational experiences – it reorients the ways in which we think about the materials, things, objects of learning, as well as who and what matters in education, and how mattering is discursively represented.

A further useful method for thinking about materiality and the relationships between things, people and spaces is the tool and research method of concept mapping (see also Chapter 8). Concept mapping has emerged within research over the past forty years or so, notably within the work of Joe Novak (2010) and more recently in the works by Ian Kinchin (2014, 2015). The aim of concept map–mediated dialogue is to surface underlying beliefs and values. However, the dialogue between researcher/participant also intertwines and is situated around the physical and visual artefact: the map, which is shared, created and adapted as the dialogue occurs. Concept mapping can be used in a multiple of ways for educational research (Gravett, Kinchin and Winstone 2020; Gravett et al. 2020). Concept mapping interviews serve as opportunities for dialogue where the process of mapping allows ideas and thoughts to be surfaced, and connections between interviewer and interviewee to develop, but it also allows these ideas to evolve alongside and through the physical paper map. Cartographic approaches, such as concept mapping, also offer helpful ways to surface the relational aspects of ideas and practices – as ideas are connected together via the nodes drawn between concepts on the map, suggesting fluidity and interconnection. As a method, then, concept mapping offers ways to help us to think both about the relationality of concepts, as well as about how ideas and materialities also work and develop together.

Another helpful method for exploring relational pedagogies, and mattering, in higher education is the method of collective biography. Two powerful examples of engaging this method are shown within the following studies: 'Grim tales: Meetings, matterings and moments of silencing and frustration in everyday academic life', and '"Working on a rocky shore": Micro-moments of positive affect in academic work', studies that have also informed other chapters of this book, for example, Chapter 6. In their book, titled *Doing Collective Biography* (2006), Bronwyn Davies and Susanne Gannon outline this meaningful method as a tool to understanding both mattering and relationships within educational contexts. In this extract, Davies and Gannon describe how collective biography deviates from other qualitative research:

> An interview can be described as the interviewee's best attempt to describe or explain, in the particular dialogic context of the interview, what he or she remembers, based on a particular history of observation and experience. Similarly, our analysis of the interview transcript is our best attempt, based on what we remember having seen or heard or read, both 'in' the data and outside the data, to make sense of what is said. Sometimes we attempt to make this sensemaking more 'scientific' by engaging in elaborate forms of coding and quantifying, or following the carefully laid out steps of a particular, recognized method, or producing elaborate transcription formats that reveal what is 'really going on'. We comfort ourselves with methodic terms like 'triangulation', hoping that if the question has been approached from three sides, surely the answer is reliable. (Davies and Gannon 2006: 1)

Here, Davies and Gannon describe the comforting, prescribed, pseudoscientific approaches of qualitative methods; in contrast, collective biography transparently acknowledges its clumsiness, situatedness and particularity. This method is not about attempts to represent a reality, or about masking approaches within the language of positivism, but about asking its participants/researchers to do something quite different. Instead, collective biography offers a flexible and creative approach to exploring collectives' lived experiences and the formation of subjectivities (Davies and Gannon 2006). Collectives work by exploring their own memories upon an agreed theme, or they may begin with identifying a concept or theory that the group wants to investigate. Gannon and colleagues describe how collective biography workshops enable colleagues to come together:

> Our disciplines and experience varied. Our interests in materiality and space led to the only instruction that preceded the workshop – take a photo on your phone of your academic life. Thus we incorporated a photo elicitation technique into our collective biography methodology. Rather than straightforward representations, we mobilised the images as provocations that we worked with laterally and affectively, writing about each other's images as well as our own. (Gannon et al. 2019: 49)

Here, the approach described offers an innovative approach for qualitative researchers who may be interested in examining the situated experiences of education and of educators, as well as thinking about new ways to understand conceptions of mattering and relations.

Any of the experimental research methods included above can be engaged together with a sociomaterial or posthuman inflected approach to think about connections, mattering and the relational in new ways. However, of course, these approaches have still been focused upon or included human participants, and there is also some innovative research being carried out to think about how we might disrupt the centrality of humans within educational research by foregrounding objects as participants. For example, Catherine Adams and Terrie Lynn Thompson (2016) and Lesley Gourlay (2021) have examined how we might conduct interviews with objects in order to enact research that aligns more closely with a posthuman approach. Adams and Thompson draw upon actor-network theory, phenomenology and other sociomaterial approaches to offer heuristics for interviewing objects: asking critical questions of a range of things in professional and personal spaces. Likewise, Gourlay (2021) conducts a series of interviews with her laptop, with a Massive Online Open Course (MOOC), a flipped classroom, and a virtual learning environment, in order to understand in new ways how objects and humans entangle, and to disrupt the primacy of the human within research practices. Clearly, both of these innovative approaches, and all of the research methods explored above, offer us new ideas to think with. Through further work we can continue to unpack what relational pedagogies might look like, and what they might mean, in education theory-practice.

Insights for Institutional Communities

Research then can be generative and can offer exciting possibilities for advancing our understanding of the relational in higher education, and how we might develop our pedagogies as a result. However, arguably, another of the key places that the impact of educational research needs to be felt is within the world of policymaking. And yet, as Gill Aitken explains in this article with Tim Fawns and colleagues (Fawns et al. 2022: 6), this can be difficult to achieve. However, Aitken's view is that what is needed is

> to bring people together to amplify our voices … we can do as much research as we like, but unless these issues are debated at the right level in institutions – until we have people who are effectively representing teachers on central university committees, and representing us authentically, so that our voices are heard – it's difficult to see how things will change.

Issues and ideas need to be taken further, and to be debated at 'the right level' within institutional hierarchies. This might be hard to achieve, but it is not impossible. As Cathy Bovill (2020a: 69) suggests, there is a 'need to support and advise senior managers in designing and implementing strategies and policies that will create a culture promoting relational pedagogy and co- creation across universities'. Bovill describes how, in work taking place at the University of Edinburgh to envision the future of university digital education, policymakers have explicitly prioritized the importance of relational pedagogies through embedding a commitment to this via policy:

> This work explicitly highlights the importance of 'prioritising human contact and relationships' and the use of co-design methodologies and enhanced student agency. If you are a senior manager within a university, you can support relational pedagogy and co-creation by making public statements like this. Even more powerful is if you can match this public statement with a commitment to resources to support the changes that are needed to make relational teaching a reality. (Bovill 2020a: 69)

Fawns et al. (2022) suggest that one answer may also be seeking out greater opportunities for dialogue between stakeholders:

> We might then ask how we can make more use of our agency to influence structures. In my view, as in our programme and teaching, relationships are key. If we are to have any hope of changing the organisational structure, we need to develop relationships with people in management positions. For this, we need to find opportunities to gain a better understanding of why others do things the way they do. (7)

Perhaps one additional aspect of relational pedagogies is the need to develop relationships with other stakeholders in and beyond institutions, in order to be able to gain resource to enact those pedagogies effectively.

Challenges and Threats to Relational Pedagogies and Pedagogies of Mattering

There are durable challenges to developing relational pedagogies in higher education that remain. As discussed, there are real disconnects that exist between stakeholders within institutions, such as educational researchers or teachers, and institutional leaders or policymakers. Another barrier may be that the language used by theorists may seem obscure and off putting, too theoretical. In her paper 'The offence of theory', Maggie Maclure (2010) explores how theory inevitably offends.

> Theory offends. Impure and indecisive, it can't be used to lift things up to higher levels of abstraction, generality or synthesis; nor boil or break them down into themes or basic categories. It is unable to make itself transparent or remove itself from the field of its own operations so that reality might speak for itself. The fascination with writing and language (in some versions) makes it seem frivolous, pretentiously literary, or the arcane preserve of an elite caste of scholars intent on preserving their own power and privilege. Policy makers and practitioners are put off by Theory's tendency to complicate, its vaunted uncertainty, and its fraught entanglement with the 'practice' that it is supposed either to explain or to serve. (278–9)

Recognizing this, this book has sought to avoid being 'pretentiously literary' in its style, but nevertheless, I appreciate that, for many, even the concept of engaging theory in practice may seem unwelcome. Maclure (2010: 280) explains that policymakers and practitioners are often 'put off by theory's tendency to complicate, its vaunted uncertainty, and its fraught entanglement with the "practice" that it is supposed either to explain or to serve'. Complexity and uncertainty may be valued by researchers, but far less so by managers and institutional leaders, and researchers will have to work hard to ensure that complex ideas can be clearly communicated. Likewise, Elizabeth Adams St Pierre (2016: 111) notes that the education sector is afflicted by an urge to 'leap to application', demanding the practical collection of data as a prelude to playing with and creating knowledge. However, like Maclure, I believe that 'the offence of theory is nevertheless productive – a necessary impediment to the recurring "desire to rejoin the simple" (Derrida 1998)' (Maclure 2010: 280).

Maclure explains that one criticism of theoretical writing is that 'often, writing on and of theory hangs in a discursive space that is fairly empty of examples, let alone the focus and challenge of a specific investigation or research project' (2010: 281). The relationship between theory and practice is complex and can be problematic. Of course, we need to acknowledge the significant voices of those policymakers, managers and practitioners who are alienated by theory's 'tendency to complicate', as well as with those who argue that theory is divorced from practice, or not meaningful for educators. Nonetheless, I believe that complexity is essential. Not all questions have simple answers. Theory does not simply serve, follow or explain practice.

Another real challenge for educators interested in engaging relational pedagogies and thoughtful teaching practices is the challenge of how concepts and ideas may be misappropriated. It is encouraging and exciting to see how pedagogies of care have become increasingly popular within higher education theory-practice in recent times, especially as an entry point to thinking about relational pedagogies. However, if concepts are adopted only superficially, then they risk contributing to the harm they were originally designed to mitigate. Discussions of caring campuses, communities and belonging are now regular phrases that can be observed in institutional discourses and the language of universities' websites and prospectuses. However, these discourses may often overlook the nuances of what care or belonging really looks and feels like. For example, how much has really changed in practice for those teachers expected to enact care? If taken simplistically, a command to care, or to care more, can be deeply troubling. Rather, there is a real need to understand how practices and pedagogies oriented to care, inclusivity and the relational in higher education contexts are marked by gender, race, (dis)ability and social inequalities (Gravett, Taylor and Fairchild 2021). This is even more of a concern given the broader social contexts in which social inequalities are widening and educational disparities remain entrenched. For example, working in universities is still a highly gendered practice and there remains 'a tiny number of women vice-chancellors, a disproportionately low number of women professors, a shamefully low number of black female professors' (Taylor and Fairchild 2020: 11). Certainly, care has long been taken for granted as 'women's work', and feminists have explored how ethics of care may be rooted in considerations of how interpersonal connections are often bound up with power. Care remains a complex, potentially problematic and ambivalent notion (Puig de la Bellacasa 2017).

These are all durable challenges that relational pedagogies need to grapple with. As Bell (2021) explains, relational pedagogies

> can be undermined, and even reversed, in some situations where we are stressed (von Dawans, Strojny, and Domes 2021). With more casualised work and increasing workloads in UK HE, stresses are increasing, possibly undermining the possibility for relational pedagogy. While universities have been spending more on new buildings as a result of the increase in tuition fees (Morris, Adams, and Ratcliffe 2016), this study indicates that students appear to be more interested in having the attention, support and care of their lecturers, than the campus facilities. If so, student satisfaction in UK HE can best be increased by providing a more supportive context for relational pedagogy through secure jobs and adequate staffing. Sensitive and caring teaching can enhance student satisfaction, in turn increasing further student recruitment and retention, and thereby providing more resources for staffing. This virtuous circle can only, function, however, if the need for relational pedagogy is properly understood and valued.

Final Thoughts

This book ends with a simple idea: teaching is a relationship. It is a relationship between students and staff, between students and peers and between staff and their colleagues, which may also usefully include insights from wider 'others' beyond educational spheres, as explored in Chapter 7. However, it is also relational in the sense that matter matters: material contexts, spaces, objects and things all entangle to impact upon the learning and teaching that happens. Mattering then is a useful word. Mobile and multiple in its meaning it can be helpful to us in reminding us that relationships matter, but so do the non-human things around us. It invites us to think beyond those well-worn cognitive, psychological and humanist tracks of thought that have dominated educational research and practice for so long.

Catherine Manathunga (2011) warns that educational research must move forward as a field if it is not in danger of becoming irrelevant in our rapidly shifting, globalized world:

> A field that does not move on to address new and intriguing, critical questions about teaching and learning and the overall purposes of higher education in society to 'know differently' as Haggis (2009) challenges us to do could be in danger of becoming irrelevant in our rapidly shifting, globalised world. We all need to think critically about how we might broaden our field to investigate new or different questions and to draw upon different theoretical paradigms and methodologies. (360)

I hope that this book has been an opportunity for you to think differently about higher education and has inspired some new ideas to take forward. My view is that relationships matter. Relations are complex and situated, and greater time, thought, and care taken to understand our environments and contexts, and how these shape teaching and learning, will pay dividends in developing our theory-practice. I have suggested that asking who and what matters within higher education, as well as acknowledging the importance of the relational, may be the first steps in moving towards creating opportunities for supporting staff to prioritize their connections with students. This might be in terms of increasing time for student–staff interactions, prioritizing the value of teaching within institutions (and providing further resourcing), attending to the diverse day-to-day practices of learning interactions, or even just creating spaces for conversations regarding relational pedagogies to take place. Teaching in higher education remains a difficult role and there are many challenges and constraints. However, interactions – or intra-actions (Barad 2007) – matter. I believe that education can also be the practice of freedom (hooks 1994), enabling others to feel that they matter, that they have something to offer and that if they wish to they can belong.

There is further work to be done to understand more about what meaningful connections for students look like and how we can find more spaces and ways in which to enact them. This is an evolving area, generating thorny questions including how we might foster connections when learning and teaching, as well as what broader sociomaterial actors might be involved in learning interactions, and how we might trace these practices, relations and assemblages. Questions include exploring further how mattering, engagement, belonging and connection are experienced by different staff and students, and in different teaching and learning contexts. They will inevitably include considering how mattering and relational pedagogies can be enacted in hybrid, digital and post-Covid learning environments, and what resources teachers might need to enact such pedagogies of mattering. Thinking about these questions might involve engaging in new kinds of educational research practices, having conversations with new or different stakeholders, or in alternative ways. It might involve thinking with different theories. I hope that the chapters in this book have offered a step forward in doing some of this work, as well as raising some new questions to think with.

References

Adams, C., and T. L. Thompson (2016), *Researching a Posthuman World: Interviews with Digital Objects*, Cham, Switzerland: Palgrave.

Advance HE (2021), 'National Teaching Fellowship'. Available online: https://www.advance-he.ac.uk/awards/teaching-excellence-awards/national-teaching-fellowship (accessed 28 June 2022).

Ahmed, S. (2004), *The Cultural Politics of Emotion*, London: Routledge.

Ahmed, S. (2012), *On Being Included: Racism and Diversity in Institutional Life*, Durham, NC: Duke University Press.

Ahmed, S. (2014), 'Selfcare as Warfare'. Available online: http://feministkilljoys.com/2014/08/25/selfcare-as-warfare/ (accessed 28 June 2022).

Ahmed, S. (2017), *Living a Feminist Life*, Durham, NC: Duke University Press.

Ahn, M. Y., and H. H. Davis (2020), 'Four Domains of Students' Sense of Belonging to University', *Studies in Higher Education*, 45 (3): 622–34.

Ajjawi, R., R. E. Olson and N. McNaughton (2021), 'Emotion as Reflexive Practice: A New Discourse for Feedback Practice and Research', *Medical Education*, 56 (5): 480–8.

Ali, X., J. Tatam, K. Gravett and I. M. Kinchin (2021), 'Partnership Values: An Evaluation of Student–Staff Research Projects at a UK Higher Education Institution', *International Journal for Students as Partners*, 5 (1): 12–25.

Badmington, N. (2003), 'Theorizing Posthumanism', *Cultural Critique*, 53: 10–27.

Balloo, K., L. Barnett, K. Gravett, X. Ali, J. Tatam and N. Winstone, 'Visualising Students' Experiences of Higher Education Assessment and Feedback Practices', forthcoming.

Bamberger, A., P. Morris and M. Yemini (2019), 'Neoliberalism, Internationalisation and Higher Education: Connections, Contradictions and Alternatives', *Discourse: Studies in the Cultural Politics of Education*, 40 (2): 203–16.

Barad, K. (2003), 'Posthumanist Performativity: Toward an Understanding of How Matter Comes to Matter', *Signs*, 28 (3): 801–31.

Barad, K. (2007), *Meeting the Universe Halfway: Quantum Physics and the Entanglement of Matter and Meaning*, Durham, NC: Duke University Press.

Barnacle, R., and G. Dall'Alba (2017), 'Committed to Learn: Student Engagement and Care in Higher Education', *Higher Education Research & Development*, 36 (7): 1326–38.

Barnett, R. (2000), 'University Knowledge in an Age of Supercomplexity', *Higher Education*, 40: 409–22.

Barnett, R. (2018), *The Ecological University: A Feasible Utopia*, London: Routledge.

Barthes, R. (1977), *Image, Music, Text*, London: Fontana.

Bauman, Z. (2000), *Liquid Modernity*, Cambridge: Polity.

Bayne, S. (2018), 'Posthumanism: A Navigation Aid for Educators', *On Education. Journal for Research and Debate*, 2 (1): 1–7.

Bayne, S., P. Evans, R. Ewins, J. Knox, J. Lamb, H. Macleod, C. O'Shea, J. Ross, P. Sheail and C. Sinclair (2020), *The Manifesto for Teaching Online*, Cambridge, MA: MIT Press.

Beard, C., S. Clegg and K. Smith (2007), 'Acknowledging the Affective in Higher Education', *British Educational Research Journal*, 33 (2): 235–52.

Bearman, M., and E. Molloy (2017), 'Intellectual Streaking: The Value of Teachers Exposing Minds (and Hearts)', *Medical Teacher*, 39 (12): 1284–5.

Bell, S., T. Berg and S. Morse (2016), *Rich Pictures: Encouraging Resilient Communities*, London: Routledge.

Bell, K. (2021), 'Increasing Undergraduate Student Satisfaction in Higher Education: The Importance of Relational Pedagogy', *Journal of Further and Higher Education*, 46 (4): 490–503.

Bell, A., and K. Thomson (2018), 'Supporting Peer Observation of Teaching: Collegiality, Conversations, and Autonomy', *Innovations in Education and Teaching International*, 55 (3): 276–84.

Benhabib, S. (1992), *Situating the Self: Gender, Community, and Postmodernism in Contemporary Ethics*, New York: Routledge.

Bennett, J. (2009), *Vibrant Matter: A Political Ecology of Things*, Durham, NC: Duke University Press.

Bergmark, U., and S. Westman (2016), 'Co-creating Curriculum in Higher Education: Promoting Democratic Values and a Multidimensional View on Learning', *International Journal for Academic Development*, 21 (1): 28–40.

Biesta, G. (2004), '"Mind the Gap!" Communication and the Educational Relation', *Counterpoints*, 259: 11–22.

Biesta, G., C. Bingham, J. N. Hutchison, B. L. McDaniel, F. Margonis, C. Mayo, C. M. Pijanowski, R. M. Romano, A. M. Sidorkin, B. S. Stengel and B. J. Thayer-Bacon (2004), 'Manifesto of Relational Pedagogy: Meeting to Learning, Learning to Meet. A Joint Contribution by All Authors', in C. Bingham and A. M. Sidorkin (eds), *No Education without Relation*, 5–9, New York: Peter Lang.

Blackmore, J. (2020), 'The Carelessness of Entrepreneurial Universities in a World Risk Society: A Feminist Reflection on the Impact of Covid-19 in Australia', *Higher Education Research and Development*, 39 (7): 1332–6.

Bottrell, D., and C. Manathunga, eds (2019), *Resisting Neoliberalism in Higher Education, Volume 1: Seeing through the Cracks*, Cham, Switzerland: Palgrave Critical University Studies.

Bovill, C. (2019), 'Student–Staff Partnerships in Learning and Teaching: An Overview of Current Practice and Discourse', *Journal of Geography in Higher Education*, 43 (4): 385–98.

Bovill, C. (2020a), *Co-creating Learning and Teaching: Towards Relational Pedagogy in Higher Education*, St Albans: Critical Publishing.

Bovill, C. (2020b), 'Co-creation in Learning and Teaching: The Case for a Whole-Class Approach in Higher Education', *Higher Education*, 79: 1023–37.

Bozalek, V., and M. Zembylas (2017), 'Towards a Response-able Pedagogy across Higher Education Institutions in Post-Apartheid South Africa: An Ethico-Political Analysis', *Education as Change*, 21 (2): 62–85.

Bozalek, V., M. Zembylas and J. C. Tronto (2021), *Posthuman and Political Care Ethics for Reconfiguring Higher Education Pedagogies*, Abingdon, Oxon: Routledge.

Bozalek, V., T. Shefer and M. Zembylas (2019), 'Response-Able (Peer) Reviewing Matters in Higher Education: A Manifesto', in C. A. Taylor and A. Bayley (eds), *Posthumanism and Higher Education: Reimagining Pedagogy, Practice and Research*, 349–57, Cham, Switzerland: Palgrave Macmillan.

Braidotti, R. (2013), *The Posthuman*, Cambridge: Polity Press.

Brantmeier, E. J. (2013), 'Pedagogy of Vulnerability: Definitions, Assumptions, and Applications', in J. Lin, R. L. Oxford and E. J. Brantmeier (eds), *Re-envisioning Higher Education: Embodied Pathways to Wisdom and Transformation*, 96–106, Charlotte, NC: Information Age.

Bright, D. (2017), 'The Pleasure of Writing: Escape from the Dominant System', in S. Riddle, M. K. Harmes and P. A. Danaher (eds), *Producing Pleasure in the Contemporary University*, 37–47, Rotterdam: Sense.

Brookfield, S. (2015), *The Skillful Teacher: On Technique, Trust, and Responsiveness in the Classroom*, 3rd edn, San Francisco: Jossey-Bass.

Brookfield, S. (2017), *Becoming a Critically Reflective Teacher*, 2nd edn, San Francisco: Jossey-Bass.

Brooks, R. (2021), 'The Construction of Higher Education Students within National Policy: A Cross-European Comparison', *Compare: A Journal of Comparative and International Education*, 51 (2): 161–80.

Brooks, R., and J. Waters (2018), *Materialities and Mobilities in Education*, London: Routledge.

Brooks, R., A. Gupta, S. Jayadeva and J. Abrahams (2020), 'Students' Views about the Purpose of Higher Education: A Comparative Analysis of Six European Countries', *Higher Education Research and Development*, 40 (7): 1375–88.

Burke, K., and S. Larmar (2020), 'Acknowledging Another Face in the Virtual Crowd: Reimagining the Online Experience in Higher Education through an Online Pedagogy of Care', *Journal of Further and Higher Education*, 45 (5): 601–15.

Burnett, C., G. Merchant and I. Guest (2021), 'What Matters to Teachers about Literacy Teaching: Exploring Teachers' Everyday/Everynight Worlds through Creative Data Visualisation', *Teaching and Teacher Education*, 107: 103480.

Cates, R. M., M. R. Madigan and V. L. Reitenauer (2018), '"Locations of Possibility": Critical Perspectives on Partnership', *International Journal for Students as Partners*, 2 (1): 33–46.

Chodorow, N. (1980), 'Gender, Relation, and Difference in Psychoanalytic Perspective', in H. Eisenstein and A. Jardine (eds), *The Future of Difference*, 3–19, Boston: G. K. Hall.

Chodorow, N. (1995), 'Gender as Personal and Cultural Construction', *Signs: Journal of Women in Culture and Society*, 20 (3): 516–44.

Clegg, S. (2009), 'Forms of Knowing and Academic Development Practice', *Studies in Higher Education*, 34 (4): 403–16.

Clegg, S. (2013), 'The Space of Academia: Privilege, Agency and the Erasure of Affect', in C. Maxwell and P. Aggleton (eds), *Privilege, Agency and Affect*, 71–87, London: Palgrave Macmillan.

Clegg, S., and S. Rowland (2010), 'Kindness in Pedagogical Practice and Academic Life', *British Journal of Sociology of Education*, 31 (6): 719–35.

Cook-Sather, A., C. Bovill and P. Felten (2014), *Engaging Students as Partners in Learning and Teaching: A Guide for Faculty*, San Francisco: Jossey-Bass.

Cook-Sather, A., E. Hong, T. Moss and A. Williamson (2021), 'Developing New Faculty Voice and Agency through Trustful, Overlapping, Faculty–Faculty and Student-Faculty Conversations', *International Journal for Academic Development*, 26 (3): 347–59.

Daniels, J., and J. Brooker (2014), 'Student Identity Development in Higher Education: Implications for Graduate Attributes and Work-Readiness', *Educational Research*, 56 (1): 65–76.

Danvers, E. (2021), 'Individualised and Instrumentalised? Critical Thinking, Students and the Optics of Possibility within Neoliberal Higher Education', *Critical Studies in Education*, 62 (5): 641–56.

Davies, B., and S. Gannon (2006), *Doing Collective Biography*, New York: McGraw Hill Education.

Deleuze, G., and F. Guattari (1987), *A Thousand Plateaus: Capitalism and Schizophrenia*, London: Continuum.

Deleuze, G. (1997), *Essays Critical and Clinical*, trans. D. W. Smith and M. A. Greco, Minneapolis: University of Minnesota Press.

Department for Education and Skills (2003), 'The Future of Higher Education'. Available online: http://www.educationengland.org.uk/documents/pdfs/2003-white-paper-higher-ed.pdf (accessed 28 June 2022).

Dervin, F. (2017), '"Don't Cry – Do Research!" The Promise of Happiness for an Academic Killjoy', in S. Riddle, M. K. Harmes and P. A. Danaher (eds), *Producing Pleasure in the Contemporary University*, 243–55, Rotterdam: Sense.

Dewey, J. (2019), *Moral Principles in Education and My Pedagogic Creed*, Gorham, ME: Myers Education Press.

Donald, D. T. (2009), 'Forts, Curriculum, and Indigenous Métissage: Imagining Decolonization of Aboriginal-Canadian Relations in Educational Contexts', *First Nations Perspectives*, 2 (1): 1–24.

Donelan, M. (2020), 'Universities Minister Calls for True Social Mobility'. A speech delivered on 1 July 2020. Available online: https://www.gov.uk/government/speeches/universities-minister-calls-for-true-social-mobility (accessed 28 June 2022).

Dwyer, R., and A. L. Black (2021) 'Reimagining the Academy: Conceptual, Theoretical, Philosophical, and Methodological Sparks', in R. Dwyer and A. L. Black (eds), *Reimagining the Academy ShiFting towards Kindness, Connection, and an Ethics of Care*, 1–16, Cham, Switzerland: Palgrave Macmillan.

Ellsworth, E. (1989), 'Why Doesn't This Feel Empowering? Working through the Repressive Myths of Critical Pedagogy', *Harvard Educational Review*, 59 (3): 297–325.

Engin, M. (2016), 'Enhancing the Status of Peer Observation through the Scholarship of Teaching and Learning', *International Journal for Academic Development*, 21 (4): 377–82.

Engin, M., and B. Priest (2014), 'Observing Teaching: A Lens for Self-Reflection', *Journal of Perspectives in Applied Academic Practice*, 2 (2): 2–9.

Fairchild, N., and C. A. Taylor (2019), 'Karen Barad', in P. Atkinson, S. Delamont, A. Cernat, J. W. Sakshaug and R. A. Williams (eds), *SAGE Research Methods Foundations*. Available online: http://methods.sagepub.com/foundations/barad-karen (accessed 12 December 2021).

Fawns, T., G. Aitken, D. Jones and K. Gravett (2022), 'Beyond Technology in Online Postgraduate Education', *Postdigital Science and Education*. https://doi.org/10.1007/s42438-021-00277-x.

Felten, P. (2020), *Relationship-Rich Education: How Human Connections Drive Success in College*, Baltimore, MD: John Hopkins University Press.

Fenwick, T., R. Edwards and P. Sawchuk (2011), *Emerging Approaches to Educational Research Tracing the Socio-material*, London: Routledge.

Finn, K. (2015), *Personal Life, Young Women and Higher Education: A Relational Approach to Student and Graduate Experiences*, London: Palgrave Macmillan.

Foucault, M. (1975), *Discipline and Punish: The Birth of the Prison*, Harmondsworth: Penguin.

Foucault, M. (1976), *The Will to Knowledge: The History of Sexuality. Volume One*, Harmondsworth: Penguin.

Fraser, M., S. Kember and C. Lury (2005), 'Inventive Life: Approaches to the New Vitalism', *Theory, Culture & Society*, 22 (1): 1–14.

Freire, P. (1968), *Pedagogy of the Oppressed*, London: Continuum.

Gannon, S., C. Taylor, G. Adams, H. Donaghue, S. Hannam-Swain, J. Harris-Evans, J. Healey and P. Moore (2019), ' "Working on a Rocky Shore": Micro-Moments of Positive Affect in Academic Work', *Emotion, Space and Society*, 31: 48–55.

Gannon, S., G. Kligte, J. MacLean, M. Perrier, E. Swan, I. Vanni and H. van Rijswijk (2015), 'Uneven Relationalities, Collective Biography and Sisterly Affect in Neoliberal Universities', *Feminist Formations*, 27 (3): 189–216.

Giddens, A. (1991), *Modernity and Self-Identity: Self and Society in the Late Modern Age*, Stanford, CA: Stanford University Press.

Gilligan, C. (1982), *In a Different Voice: Psychological Theory and Women's Development*, Cambridge, MA: Harvard University Press.

Gilligan, C. (1987), 'Moral Orientation and Moral Development', in E. Feder Kittay and D. T. Meyers (eds), *Women and Moral Theory*, 19–33, Lanham, MD: Rowman & Littlefield.

Giroux, H. A. (1983), *Theory and Resistance in Education: A Pedagogy for the Opposition*, London: Heinemann.

Gosling, D. (2014), 'Collaborative Peer-Supported Review of Teaching', in J. Sachs and M. Parsell (eds), *Peer Review of Learning and Teaching in Higher Education: Professional Learning and Development in Schools and Higher Education*, 13–31, Dordrecht: Springer.

Gourlay, L. (2015), '"Student Engagement" and the Tyranny of Participation', *Teaching in Higher Education*, 20 (4): 402–11.

Gourlay, L. (2017), 'Student Engagement, "Learnification" and the Sociomaterial: Critical Perspectives on Higher Education Policy', *Higher Education Policy*, 30 (1): 23–34.

Gourlay, L. (2021), *Posthumanism and the Digital University*, London: Bloomsbury.

Gourlay, L., and M. Oliver (2016), 'Multimodal Longitudinal Journaling', in C. Haythornthwaite, R. Andrews, J. Fransman and E. M. Meyers (eds), *The SAGE Handbook of E-learning Research*, 291–312, London: SAGE.

Gourlay, L., and M. Oliver (2018), *Student Engagement in the Digital University: Sociomaterial Assemblages*, London: Routledge.

Gouwens, J., and K. P. King (2017), 'From Frustration to Flow: Finding Joy through Co-teaching', in S. Riddle, M. K. Harmes and P. A. Danaher (eds), *Producing Pleasure in the Contemporary University*, 213–27, Rotterdam: Sense.

Gravett, K. (2020), 'Feedback Literacies as Sociomaterial Practice', *Critical Studies in Education*, 63 (2): 61–274.

Gravett, K. (2021), 'Troubling Transitions and Celebrating Becomings: From Pathway to Rhizome', *Studies in Higher Education*, 46 (8): 1506–17.

Gravett, K., and R. Ajjawi (2021), 'Belonging as Situated Practice', *Studies in Higher Education*. https://doi.org/10.1080/03075079.2021.1894118.

Gravett, K., P. Baughan, N. Rao and I. M. Kinchin (2022), 'Spaces and Places for Connection in the Postdigital University', *Postdigital Science and Education*. https://doi.org/10.1007/s42438-022-00317-0.

Gravett, K., and I. M. Kinchin (2020), 'Revisiting "A 'Teaching Excellence' for the Times We Live in": Posthuman Possibilities', *Teaching in Higher Education*, 25 (8): 1028–34.

Gravett, K., I. M. Kinchin and N. E. Winstone (2020), '"More Than Customers": Conceptions of Students as Partners Held by Students, Staff, and Institutional Leaders', *Studies in Higher Education*, 45 (12): 2574–87.

Gravett, K., I. M. Kinchin, N. E. Winstone, K. Balloo, M. Heron, A. Hosein, S. Lygo-Baker and E. Medland (2020), 'The Development of Academics' Feedback Literacy: Experiences of Learning from Critical Feedback via Scholarly Peer Review', *Assessment and Evaluation in Higher Education*, 45 (5): 651–65.

Gravett, K., and N. E. Winstone (2019), '"Feedback Interpreters": The Role of Learning Development Professionals in Facilitating University Students' Engagement with Feedback', *Teaching in Higher Education*, 24 (6): 723–38.

Gravett, K., and N. E. Winstone (2020), 'Making Connections: Alienation and Authenticity within Students' Relationships in Higher Education', *Higher Education Research and Development*. https://doi.org/10.1080/07294360.2020.1842335.

Gravett, K., C. A. Taylor and N. Fairchild (2021), 'Pedagogies of Mattering: Re-conceptualising Relational Pedagogies in Higher Education', *Teaching in Higher Education*. https://doi.org/10.1080/13562517.2021.1989580.

Gravett, K., N. Yakovchuk and I. M. Kinchin, eds (2020), *Enhancing Student-Centred Teaching in Higher Education: The Landscape of Student–Staff Partnerships*, Cham, Switzerland: Palgrave Macmillan.

Groves, O., and S. O'Shea (2019), 'Learning to "Be" a University Student: First in Family Students Negotiating Membership of the University Community', *International Journal of Educational Research*, 98: 48–54.

Guerin, C. (2013), 'Rhizomatic Research Cultures, Writing Groups and Academic Researcher Identities', *International Journal of Doctoral Studies*, 8: 137–50.

Guitman, R., A. Acai and L. Mercer-Mapstone (2020), 'Unlearning Hierarchies and Striving for Relational Diversity: A Feminist Manifesto for Student–Staff Partnerships', in L. Mercer-Mapstone and S. Abbot (eds), *The Power of Partnership: Students, Faculty, and Staff Revolutionizing Higher Education*, 61–72, Elon, NC: Elon University Center for Engaged Learning.

Haraway, D. J. (1988), 'Situated Knowledges: The Science Question in Feminism and the Privilege of Partial Perspective', *Feminist Studies*, 14 (3): 575–99.

Haraway, D. J. (1997), Modest_Witness@Second_Millennium. *FemaleMan_Meets_OncoMouse™: Feminism and Technoscience*, Abingdon: Routledge.

Harvey, D. (2005), *A Brief History of Neoliberalism*, Oxford: Oxford University Press.

Hay, D. B., I. M. Kinchin and S. Lygo-Baker (2008), 'Making Learning Visible: The Role of Concept Mapping in Higher Education', *Studies in Higher Education*, 33 (3): 295–311.

Healey, M., A. Flint and K. Harrington (2014), *Engagement through Partnership: Students as Partners in Learning and Teaching in Higher Education*, New York: Higher Education Academy. Available online: https://www. heacademy.ac.uk/engagement-through-partnership-students-partners-learning-andteaching-higher-education (accessed 12 March 2020).

Healey, M., K. E. Matthews and A. Cook-Sather (2020), *Writing about Learning and Teaching in Higher Education*, Elon, NC: Elon University Center for Engaged Learning. https://www.centerforengagedlearning.org/books/writing-about-learning/.

Heffernan, T. (2021), 'Sexism, Racism, Prejudice, and Bias: A Literature Review and Synthesis of Research Surrounding Student Evaluations of Courses and Teaching',

Assessment & Evaluation in Higher Education. https://doi.org/10.1080/02602 938.2021.1888075.

Heron, M., K. Gravett and N. Yakovchuk (2021), 'Publishing and Flourishing: Writing for Desire in Higher Education', *Higher Education Research and Development*, 40 (3): 538–51.

Hickey-Moody, A., C. Horn, M. Willcox and E. Florence (2021), *Arts-Based Methods for Research with Children*, Cham, Switzerland: Palgrave Macmillan.

Honan, E. (2017), 'Producing Moments of Pleasure within the Confines of the Neoliberal University', in S. Riddle, M. K. Harmes and P. A. Danaher (eds), *Producing Pleasure in the Contemporary University*, 13–24, Leiden: Sense.

hooks, b. (1994), *Teaching to Transgress: Education as the Practice of Freedom*, London: Routledge.

Ingleby, E. (2015), 'The House That Jack Built: Neoliberalism, Teaching in Higher Education and the Moral Objections', *Teaching in Higher Education*, 20 (5): 518–29.

Jauhiainen, A., A. Jauhiainen and A. Laiho (2009), 'The Dilemmas of the "Efficiency University" Policy and the Everyday Life of University Teachers', *Teaching in Higher Education*, 14 (4): 417–28.

Kahu, E. R., and K. Nelson (2018), 'Student Engagement in the Educational Interface: Understanding the Mechanisms of Student Success', *Higher Education Research and Development*, 37 (1): 58–71.

Kandiko Howson, C., and S. Weller (2016), 'Defining Pedagogic Expertise: Students and New Lecturers as Co-developers in Learning and Teaching', *Teaching Learning Inquiry* 4 (2): 50–63.

Kimmerer, R. W. (2020), *Braiding Sweetgrass: Indigenous Wisdom, Scientific Knowledge and the Teachings of Plants*, London: Penguin.

Kinchin, I. M. (2014), 'Concept Mapping as a Learning Tool in Higher Education: A Critical Analysis of Recent Reviews', *Journal of Continuing Higher Education*, 62 (1): 39–49.

Kinchin, I. M. (2015), 'Novakian Concept Mapping in University and Professional Education', *Knowledge Management & E-Learning*, 7 (1): 1–5.

Kinchin, I. M. (2019), 'Care as a Threshold Concept for Teaching in the Salutogenic University', *Teaching in Higher Education*, 27 (2): 171–84.

Kinchin, I. M., and K. Gravett (2022), *Dominant Discourses in Higher Education: Critical Perspectives, Cartographies and Practice*, London: Bloomsbury.

Kinchin, I. M., and N. E. Winstone (2017), *Pedagogic Frailty and Resilience in the University*, Rotterdam: Sense.

Kneebone, R. (2020), *Expert: Understanding the Path to Mastery*, Harmondsworth: Penguin.

Kneebone, R., and C. Schlegel (2021), 'Thinking across Disciplinary Boundaries in a Time of Crisis', *The Lancet* 397 (10269): 89–90.

Kreber, C. (2010), 'Academics' Teacher Identities, Authenticity and Pedagogy', *Studies in Higher Education*, 35: 171–94.

Kreber, C., M. Klampfleitner, V. McCune, S. Bayne and M. Knottenbelt (2007), 'What Do You Mean by "Authentic"? A Comparative Review of the Literature on Conceptions of Authenticity in Teaching', *Adult Education Quarterly*, 58 (1): 22–43.

Latour, B. (2005), *Reassembling the Social: An Introduction to Actor-Network Theory*, Oxford: Oxford University Press.

Lave, J., and E. Wenger (1991), *Situated Learning. Legitimate Peripheral Participation*, Cambridge: Cambridge University Press.

Leathwood, C. (2006), 'Gender, Equity and the Discourse of the Independent Learner in Higher Education', *Higher Education*, 52 (4): 611–33.

Liebenberg, L. (2018), 'Thinking Critically about Photovoice: Achieving Empowerment and Social Change', *International Journal of Qualitative Methods*, 17 (1): 1–9.

Loch, S., L. Henderson and E. Honan (2017), 'The Joy in Writing Assemblage', in S. Riddle, M. K. Harmes and P. A. Danaher (eds), *Producing Pleasure in the Contemporary University*, 65–79, Leiden: Sense.

Lorde, A. (1988), *A Burst of Light: Essays*, Ithaca, NY: Firebrand Books.

Lumb, M., and P. J. Burke (2019), 'Re/cognising the Discursive Fr/Ames of Equity and Widening Participation in Higher Education', *International Studies in Sociology of Education*, 28 (3–4): 215–36.

Lygo-Baker, S., I. M. Kinchin and N. E. Winstone (2019), *Engaging Student Voices in Higher Education: Diverse Perspectives and Expectations in Partnership*, Cham, Switzerland: Palgrave Macmillan.

Macfarlane, B. (2016), 'Collegiality and Performativity in a Competitive Academic Culture', *Higher Education Review*, 48 (2): 31–50.

Macfarlane, B., and L. Gourlay (2009), 'The Reflection Game: Enacting the Penitent Self', *Teaching in Higher Education*, 14 (4): 455–59.

Macfarlane, B., and M. Tomlinson (2017), 'Critical and Alternative Perspectives on Student Engagement', *Higher Education Policy*, 30: 1–4.

MacLure, M. (2010), 'The Offence of Theory', *Journal of Education Policy*, 25 (2): 277–86.

Macmurray, J. (1964), 'Teachers and Pupils', *Educational Forum*, 29 (1): 17–24.

Manathunga, C. (2011), 'The Field of Educational Development: Histories and Critical Questions', *Studies in Continuing Education*, 33 (3): 347–62.

Manathunga, C., and D. Bottrell (2019), *Resisting Neoliberalism in Higher Education, Volume II: Prising Open the Cracks*, Cham, Switzerland: Palgrave Critical University Studies.

Mangione, D., and L. Norton (2020), 'Problematising the Notion of "the Excellent Teacher": Daring to Be Vulnerable in Higher Education', *Teaching in Higher Education*.

Martínez, R. S., R. G. Floyd and L. W. Erichsen (2011), 'Strategies and Attributes of Highly Productive Scholars and Contributors to the School Psychology

Literature: Recommendations for Increasing Scholarly Productivity', *Journal of School Psychology*, 49 (6): 691–720.

Massey, D. (1994), *Space, Place and Gender*, Cambridge: Polity Press.

Massey, D. (1999), *Power-Geometries and the Politics of Space-Time*, Heidelberg: University of Heidelberg Press.

Massey, D. (2005), *For Space*, London: Sage.

Matthews, K. E., A. Dwyer, S. Russell and E. Enright (2019), 'It Is a Complicated Thing: Leaders' Conceptions of Students as Partners in the Neoliberal University', *Studies in Higher Education*, 44 (12): 2196–207.

Matthews, K. E., A. Cook-Sather and M. Healey. (2018), 'Connecting Learning, Teaching, and Research through Student–Staff Partnerships: Toward Universities as Egalitarian Learning Communities', in V. Tong, A. Standen and M. Sotiriou (eds), *Research Equals Teaching: Inspiring Research-Based Education through Student–Staff Partnerships*, 23–9, London: University College of London Press.

May, V. (2016), 'When Recognition Fails: Mass Observation Project Accounts of Not Belonging', *Sociology*, 50 (4): 748–63.

McCandless, D. (2010), *Information Is Beautiful*, London: Collins.

Mercer-Mapstone, L., and C. Bovill (2020), 'Equity and Diversity in Institutional Approaches to Student–Staff Partnership Schemes in Higher Education', *Studies in Higher Education*, 45 (12): 2541–57.

Mercer-Mapstone, L., and G. Mercer (2018), 'A Dialogue between Partnership and Feminism: Deconstructing Power and Exclusion in Higher Education', *Teaching in Higher Education*, 23 (1): 137–43.

Mercer-Mapstone, L., M. Islam and T. Reid (2021) 'Are We Just Engaging "The Usual Suspects"? Challenges in and Practical Strategies for Supporting Equity and Diversity in Student–Staff Partnership Initiatives', *Teaching in Higher Education*, 26 (2): 227–45.

Mercer-Mapstone, L., S. L. Dvorakova, K. E. Matthews, S. Abbot, B. Cheng, P. Felten, K. Knorr, E. Marquis, R. Shammas and K. Swaim (2017), 'A Systematic Literature Review of Students as Partners in Higher Education', *International Journal for Students as Partners*, 1 (1).

Meyerhoff, E. (2019), *Beyond Education: Radical Studying for Another World*, Minneapolis: University of Minnesota Press.

Mihai, A. (2021), 'The Power of Two: Exploring Co-teaching', *The Educationalist*. Available online: https://educationalist.substack.com/p/the-power-of-two-exploring-co-teaching (accessed 12 December 2021).

Miller, D. (2010), *Stuff*, London: Polity.

Mkhize, N., Q. Maqabuka and B. Magoqwana (2021), 'Pedagogy of Incoko: Challenges in Adapting Conversational Forms as a Praxis of Student Care and Engagement in the Context of Digital Learning in South Africa', *Anthropology Southern Africa*, 44 (3): 109–22.

Molloy, E., and M. Bearman (2018), 'Embracing the Tension between Vulnerability and Credibility: "Intellectual Candour" in Health Professions Education', *Medical Education*, 53 (1): 32–41.

Mountz, A., A. Bonds, B. Mansfield, J. Loyd, J. Hyndman, M. Walton-Roberts, R. Basu, R. Whitson, R. Hawkins, T. Hamilton and W. Curran (2015), 'For Slow Scholarship: A Feminist Politics of Resistance through Collective Action in the Neoliberal University', *ACME: An International Journal for Critical Geographies*, 14 (4): 1235–59.

Murphy, M. (2015), 'Unsettling Care: Troubling Transnational Itineraries of Care in Feminist Health Practices', *Social Studies of Science*, 45 (5): 717–37.

Naidoo, R., and J. Williams (2015), 'The Neoliberal Regime in English Higher Education: Charters, Consumers and the Erosion of the Public Good', *Critical Studies in Education*, 56 (2): 208–23.

National Survey of Student Engagement (NSSE) (2003), Converting Data into Action: Expanding the Boundaries of Institutional Improvement: National Survey of Student Engagement 2003 Annual Report, Bloomington: Indiana University Center for Postsecondary Research and Planning.

Newcomb, M. (2021), 'The Emotional Labour of Academia in the Time of a Pandemic: A Feminist Reflection', *Qualitative Social Work*, 20 (1–2): 639–44.

Noddings, N. (1986), *Caring: A Feminine Approach to Ethics and Moral Education*, Berkeley: University of California Press.

Noddings, N. (2005), *The Challenge to Care in Schools: An Alternative Approach to Education*, New York: Teachers College Press.

Noddings, N. (2012), 'The Caring Relation in Teaching', *Oxford Review of Education*, 38: 771–81.

Novak, J. D. (2010), *Learning, Creating and Using Knowledge: Concept Maps as Facilitative Tools in Schools and Corporations*, 2nd edn, Oxford: Routledge.

Nxumalo, F. (2020), 'Place-Based Disruptions of Humanism, Coloniality and Anti-Blackness in Early Childhood Education', *Critical Studies in Teaching and Learning*, 8: 34–49.

Nxumalo, F. (2021), 'Centering Place in Early Childhood Literacies: Thinking with Black Geographies', *Research in the Teaching of English*, 56 (1): 109–11.

Olssen, M. (2016), 'Neoliberal Competition in Higher Education Today: Research, Accountability and Impact', *British Journal of Sociology of Education*, 37 (1): 129–48.

O'Shea, S. (2020), 'Crossing Boundaries: Rethinking the Ways That First-in-Family Students Navigate "Barriers" to Higher Education', *British Journal of Sociology of Education*, 41 (1): 95–110.

O'Shea, S. (2021), ' "Kids from Here Don't Go to Uni": Considering First in Family Students' Belonging and Entitlement within the Field of Higher Education', *European Journal of Education Special Issue: Higher Education Access, Participation and Progression: Inequalities of Opportunity*, 56 (1): 65–77.

Palmer, P. J. (1983), *To Know as We Are Known: Education as a Spiritual Journey*, San Francisco: Harper.

Palmer, P. J. (1998), *The Courage to Teach: Exploring the Inner Landscape of a Teacher's Life*, San Francisco: Jossey-Bass.

Palmer, P. J. (1999), *The Courage to Teach Guide for Reflection and Renewal*, with M. Scribner, San Francisco: Jossey-Bass.

Paltridge, B., and Starfield, S. (2016), *Getting Published in Academic Journals: Navigating the Publication Process*, Ann Arbor: University of Michigan Press.

Pedersen, H. (2015), 'Education and Posthumanism'. Available online: http://criticalposthumanism.net/genealogy/education/ (accessed 12 December 2021).

Peel, D. (2005), 'Peer Observation as a Transformatory Tool?' *Teaching in Higher Education*, 10 (4): 489–504.

Pounder, J. S., E. Ho Hung-lam and J. May Groves (2016), 'Faculty-Student Engagement in Teaching Observation and Assessment: A Hong Kong Initiative', *Assessment & Evaluation in Higher Education*, 41 (8): 1193–205.

Puig de la Bellacasa, M. (2017), *Matters of Care: Speculative Ethics in More Than Human Worlds*, Minneapolis: University of Minnesota Press.

Quinlan, K. (2016), *How Higher Education Feels: Commentaries on Poems That Illuminate Emotions in Learning and Teaching*, Rotterdam: Sense.

Ramezanzadeh, A., G. Zareian, S. M. R. Adel and R. Ramezanzadeh (2017), 'Authenticity in Teaching: A Constant Process of Becoming', *Higher Education*, 73: 299–315.

Rickard, C. M., M. R. McGrail, R. Jones, P. O'Meara, A. Robinson, M. Burley and G. Ray-Barruel (2009), 'Supporting Academic Publication: Evaluation of a Writing Course Combined with Writers' Support Group', *Nurse Education Today*, 29 (5): 516–21.

Riddle, S., M. K. Harmes and P. A. Danaher (eds) (2017), *Producing Pleasure in the Contemporary University*, Rotterdam: Sense.

Rose, G. (1997), 'Spatialities of "Community", Power and Change: The Imagined Geographies of Community Arts Projects', *Cultural Studies*, 11 (1): 1–16.

Rowlands, J., and S. Rawolle (2013), 'Neoliberalism Is Not a Theory of Everything: A Bourdieuian Analysis of Illusio in Educational Research', *Critical Studies in Education*, 54 (3): 260–72.

Sabri, D. (2010), 'Absence of the Academic from Higher Education Policy', *Journal of Education Policy*, 25 (2): 191–205.

Schwarz, H. L. (2019), *Connected Teaching: Relationship, Power, and Mattering in Higher Education*, Sterling, VA: Stylus.

Semetsky, I. (2011), 'Becoming-Other: Developing the Ethics of Integration', *Policy Futures in Education*, 9 (1): 138–44.

Sermijn, J., P. Devlieger and G. Loots (2008), 'The Narrative Construction of the Self: Selfhood as a Rhizomatic Story', *Qualitative Inquiry*, 14 (4): 632–50.

Shields, S. (2015), '"My Work Is Bleeding": Exploring Students' Emotional Responses to First-Year Assignment Feedback', *Teaching in Higher Education*, 20 (6): 614–24.

Smith, K. (2008), 'Who Do You Think You're Talking To? The Discourse of Learning and Teaching Strategies', *Higher Education*, 56 (4): 395–406.

Stengers, I. (2018), *Another Science Is Possible: A Manifesto for Slow Science*, Cambridge: Polity.

Stone, C., and S. O'Shea (2019), 'Older, Online and First: Recommendations for Retention and Success', *Australasian Journal of Educational Technology*, 35 (1): 57–69.

St Pierre, E. A. (2015), '"Do the Next Thing": An Interview with Elizabeth Adams St. Pierre on Post-Qualitative Methodology', *Reconceptualizing Educational Research Methodology*, 6 (1): 15–22.

St. Pierre, E. A. (2016), 'The Empirical and the New Empiricisms', *Cultural Studies ↔ Critical Methodologies*, 16 (2): 111–24.

Strayhorn, T. L. (2012), *College Students' Sense of Belonging: A Key to Educational Success for All Students*, New York: Routledge.

Sword, H., E. Trofimova and M. Ballard (2018), 'Frustrated Academic Writers', *Higher Education Research & Development*, 37 (4): 852–67.

Taylor, C. A. (2017), 'For Hermann: How Do I Love Thee? Let Me Count the Ways. Or, What My Dog Has Taught Me about a Post-Personal Academic Life', in S. Riddle, M. K. Harmes and P. A. Danaher (eds), *Producing Pleasure in the Contemporary University*, 107–19, Rotterdam: Sense.

Taylor, C. A. (2018), 'Edu-crafting Posthumanist Adventures in/for Higher Education: A Speculative Musing', *Parallax*, 24 (3): 371–81.

Taylor, C. A. (2019), 'Unfolding: Co-conspirators, Contemplations, Complications and More', in C. A. Taylor and A. Bayley (eds), *Posthumanism and Higher Education: Reimagining Pedagogy, Practice and Research*, 1–28, Cham, Switzerland: Palgrave Macmillan.

Taylor, C. A. (2020), 'Slow Singularities for Collective Mattering: New Material Feminist Praxis in the Accelerated Academy', *Irish Educational Studies*, 39 (2): 255–72.

Taylor, C. A., and C. Robinson (2009), 'Student Voice: Theorising Power and Participation', *Pedagogy Culture and Society*, (2): 161–75.

Taylor, C. A., and J. Harris-Evans (2018), 'Reconceptualising Transition to Higher Education with Deleuze and Guattari', *Studies in Higher Education*, 43 (7): 1254–67.

Taylor, C. A., and N. Fairchild (2020), 'Towards a Posthumanist Institutional Ethnography: Viscous Matterings and Gendered Bodies', *Ethnography and Education*.

Taylor, C., S. Gannon, G. Adams, H. Donaghue, S. Hannam-Swain, J. Harris-Evans, J. Healey and P. Moore (2020), 'Grim Tales: Meetings, Matterings and Moments of Silencing and Frustration in Everyday Academic Life', *International Journal of Educational Research*, 99: 101513.

The Care Collective (2020), *The Care Manifesto: The Politics of Interdependence*, London: Verso.
Thompson, M. B. (2015), 'Authenticity in Education: From Narcissism and Freedom to the Messy Interplay of Self-Exploration and Acceptable Tension', *Studies in Philosophy and Education*, 34 (6): 603–18.
Tight, M. P. (2020), 'Student Retention and Engagement in Higher Education', *Journal of Further and Higher Education*, 44 (5): 689–704.
Tinto, V. (2017), 'Reflections on Student Persistence', *Student Success*, 8 (2): 1–8.
Todd, Z. (2016), 'An Indigenous Feminist's Take on the Ontological Turn: "Ontology" Is Just Another Word for Colonialism', *Journal of Historical Sociology*, 29: 4–22.
Tronto, J. (1993), *Moral Boundaries: A Political Argument for an Ethic of Care*, London: Routledge.
Tronto, J. C. (2015), *Who Cares?: How to Reshape a Democratic Politics*, Ithaca, NY: Cornell University Press.
Tynan, L. (2021), 'What Is Relationality? Indigenous Knowledges, Practices and Responsibilities with Kin', *Cultural Geographies*, 28 (4): 1–14.
Waight, E. (2020), 'Using Photovoice to Explore Students' Study Practices', in H. Kara and S. Khoo (eds), *Researching in the Age of COVID-19, Volume 3: Creativity and Ethics*, 180–9, Bristol: Bristol University Press.
Walker-Gleaves, C. (2019), 'Is Caring Pedagogy Really So Progressive? Exploring the Conceptual and Practical Impediments to Operationalizing Care in Higher Education', in P. Gibbs and A. Peterson (eds), *Higher Education and Hope: Institutional, Pedagogical and Personal Possibilities*, 93–112, London: Palgrave Macmillan.
Wass, R., V. Anderson, R. Rabello, C. Golding, A. Rangi and E. Eteuati (2020), 'Photovoice as a Research Method for Higher Education Research', *Higher Education Research and Development*, 39 (4): 834–50.
Watermeyer, R. (2019), *Competitive Accountability in Academic Life: The Struggle for Social Impact and Public Legitimacy*, Cheltenham: Elgar.
Watermeyer, R., and M. Tomlinson (2021), 'Competitive Accountability and the Dispossession of Academic Identity: Haunted by an Impact Phantom', *Educational Philosophy and Theory*, 54 (5): 1–15.
Watts, V. (2013), 'Indigenous Place-Thought & Agency amongst Humans and Non-Humans (First Woman and Sky Woman Go on a European World Tour!)', *Decolonization: Indigeneity, Education & Society*, 2 (1): 20–34.
Whatmore, S. (1997), 'Dissecting the Autonomous Self: Hybrid Cartographies for a Relational Ethics', *Environment and Planning D: Society and Space*, 15 (1): 37–54.
Whatmore, S. (2002), *Hybrid Geographies: Natures, Cultures, Spaces*, London: Sage.
Wildcat, D. (2013), 'Introduction: Climate Change and Indigenous Peoples of the USA', *An Interdisciplinary, International Journal Devoted to the Description, Causes and Implications of Climatic Change*, 120 (3): 509–15.

Wilkins, A., and P. J. Burke (2015), 'Widening Participation in Higher Education: The Role of Professional and Social Class Identities and Commitments', *British Journal of Sociology of Education*, 36 (3): 434–52.

Wilson, S. (2016), 'Using Indigenist Research to Shape Our Future', in M. Gray, J. Coates, M. Yellow Bird and T. Hetherington (eds), *Decolonizing Social Work*, 4–5, New York: Routledge.

Wimpenny, K., and M. Savin-Baden Katherine (2013), 'Alienation, Agency and Authenticity: A Synthesis of the Literature on Student Engagement', *Teaching in Higher Education*, 18 (3): 311–26.

Winstone, N., K. Balloo, K. Gravett, D. Jacobs and H. Keen (2020), 'Who Stands to Benefit? Wellbeing, Belonging and Challenges to Equity in Engagement in Extra-Curricular Activities at University', *Active Learning in Higher Education*.

Yuval-Davis, N. (2006), 'Belonging and the Politics of Belonging', *Patterns of Prejudice*, 40 (3): 197–214.

Zepke, N., and L. Leach (2010), 'Improving Student Engagement: Ten Proposals for Action', *Active Learning in Higher Education*, 11 (3): 167–77.

Index

academic development 43, 77, 89
actor-network theory 13–14, 32, 143
affirmative ethics 75, 146, 112
agency 11, 16, 22, 27–9, 126, 130
   collective 115
   student 69, 159
   of things 2, 11, 18, 32, 75, 92–3, 95, 140
Ahmed, Sara 12, 84–5, 92–3, 115, 120, 146
arts-informed research 135, 137, 156
assemblages 14–15, 32, 64, 88, 90, 126–9, 131, 134–7, 140, 147, 149, 154, 163
assessment 73, 127–9, 131, 149
authenticity 48–9, 51–65

Barad, Karen 2, 12–13, 21, 97, 106, 131
   see also intra-action
becoming 18, 53–4, 109–22
belonging 132–40, 155–6, 161, 163
Bennett, Jane 2, 64, 92
   see also thing-power
Biesta, Gert 7, 8, 15
Bovill, Cathy 9, 68–9, 73, 76–7, 79, 142–3, 159
Brookfield, Stephen 7–8, 39–65

care 10–12, 64, 69, 76, 78, 114–16, 148–50
   pedagogies of care 106, 161–3
   see also ethic of care
   see also self-care
co-creation *see* student-staff partnerships
collective biography 84, 157–8
communities of practice 91, 106–7
concept mapping 90, 117–19, 156–7
critical pedagogy 6, 30, 56, 68
curriculum 7, 73, 75

Deleuze, Gilles 54, 109, 110–13, 119–20
dialogue 6, 118, 133–5, 156–7, 160
   between staff and students 53, 55–6, 72
digital university 13, 47, 50, 164

emotions 8–10, 85–6, 142, 146–7, 150
employability 25, 29–30, 39
engagement, student 10, 13, 39, 43, 49, 53–4, 71–5, 130–4, 146, 154
entanglement 2–3, 11–14, 18, 32–3, 85–6, 87–8, 92, 95, 106, 130–1, 134, 138, 145–8, 155, 158
ethic of Care 8, 33, 90–1, 109, 111–17, 162

feedback 62, 71, 86, 116, 127–31, 147
   peer reviewer feedback 42–3, 90–1
feminist theory 69, 84, 92, 109, 112–15, 143–4, 162
Fenwick, Tara 14, 32, 49, 125–7, 131, 139
Freire, Paulo 6, 61, 68–9

Gannon, Susanne 5, 10, 31, 83–7, 95, 143–4, 157–8
Gourlay, Lesley 14, 32, 48–9, 130–1, 154, 158

Haraway, Donna 13, 146, 148
hooks, bell 5–6, 65, 68, 74, 92, 132, 163

identity 12, 16
   student identity 25–7
   teacher identity 7, 37, 50, 53–4, 62, 64, 110
inclusivity 61, 67, 73–5, 77, 79, 136, 138, 142–3, 150, 161
individualism 3–4, 28–9, 57, 76, 90, 125, 145
integrity 1, 7, 37–8, 44, 49, 53, 110
intra-action 2, 13, 21, 52, 97, 106, 131, 145, 163

Kinchin, Ian 10, 27, 118, 156
Kneebone, Roger 98–9, 105–7

linearity 111, 113
Lorde, Audre 114–15
Lygo-Baker, Simon 27, 43, 46, 98–105

Macfarlane, Bruce 48–9, 67, 76, 79, 83, 130
marketization 4, 11, 22, 27, 48, 115
micro-moment 31, 83, 85–9, 91–2, 95, 120, 133–4

neoliberalism 3–4, 10–11, 18, 21–5, 28–33, 70, 111, 147
Noddings, Nel 8–9, 52, 109, 113

Others 13, 69, 78, 97–107

Palmer, Parker 3, 7, 37–8, 45, 53–4, 107, 109–10, 147
partnership
  see student-staff partnership
pedagogic frailty 10, 119
pedagogies of mattering 15, 114, 148–50, 160, 164
pedagogy of grace 57, 63, 65
peer observation 115–17
peer review 42, 90–1, 118
performativity 10, 22, 38, 63
photovoice 86, 134, 154–5
playful learning 135–6
postdigital 133, 164
posthumanism 3–4, 12–13, 15, 31–3, 51, 114, 120, 125, 131, 146, 158
power 9, 22, 51, 64, 75, 85–8, 91–5, 112–14, 148, 160, 162
  empowerment 28–9, 55, 60, 69
  power relations 1, 38–45, 53, 55–7, 60–1, 64, 77–8, 105, 142–3, 148, 154
  of space 132, 74
  see also thing-power

racism 31, 58–9, 62
research methods 84, 86, 127, 131, 134, 137, 153–9
response-ability 146

rhizomatic
  researchers 112, 117
  thinking 109, 112–13, 117

self-care 53, 109, 115
situated knowledges 7–8, 13–14, 21–2, 65, 131, 141, 146, 148
slow scholarship 111, 114, 115
sociomateriality 3, 13–15, 31–3, 47–9, 123–140, 154–8
St. Pierre, Elizabeth Adams 19, 121, 161
student
  centred 10, 49, 57, 150
  experience 26–7, 32, 150
  satisfaction 27, 70, 162
  student engagement, *see* Engagement
  voice 26, 28, 55, 78
student-staff partnership 10, 17, 27, 67–79, 116, 127, 147
students as partners
  see Student-staff partnership

Taylor, Carol 4, 25, 29, 31–2, 55, 65, 84, 106, 112, 114, 120–1, 126
teaching
  excellence 48, 50
  Team teaching or co-teaching 57, 91
thing power 73, 118, 126, 128
  see also Bennett, Jane
timescapes 111, 129
Todd, Zoe 15, 106, 143–4, 150
transition 27, 111, 119, 142
trust 48, 51–65, 71–2, 77, 86, 103, 147

uncertainty 39–40, 44, 102, 160–1
undergraduate education 10, 52, 127, 131, 154–5
undergraduate research 10, 52, 127, 154–5

vulnerability 37–50, 62–3, 147

white supremacy 58–9
widening participation 28, 79
Winstone, Naomi 10, 27, 43, 52
writing practices 88–9, 90, 95, 112, 118–20

www.ingramcontent.com/pod-product-compliance
Lightning Source LLC
Chambersburg PA
CBHW061834300426
44115CB00013B/2382